Y0-DDO-210

THE ETHICAL DISCOURSE OF CHINESE CHILDREN

A Narrative Approach to the Social and Moral Intricacy of Lying About Good Deeds

The Ethical Discourse of Chinese Children

A Narrative Approach to the Social and Moral Intricacy of Lying About Good Deeds

Minghui Gao

With a Foreword by
David Perkins

The Edwin Mellen Press
Lewiston•Queenston•Lampeter

Library of Congress Cataloging-in-Publication Data

Gao, Minghui.
The ethical discourse of Chinese children : a narrative approach to the social and moral intricacy of lying about good deeds / Minghui Gao ; with a foreword by David Perkins.
p. cm.
Includes bibliographical references and index.
ISBN-13: 978-0-7734-3632-9
ISBN-10: 0-7734-3632-4
1. Children--China. 2. Child rearing--China. 3. Truthfulness and falsehood--China--Psychological aspects. 4. Education--Moral and ethical values--China. 5. Social values--China. I. Title.
HQ792.C5G36 2010
305.2310951--dc22

2010015785

hors série.

A CIP catalog record for this book is available from the British Library.

The Edwin Mellen Press
Box 450
Lewiston, New York
USA 14092-0450

The Edwin Mellen Press
Box 67
Queenston, Ontario
CANADA L0S 1L0

The Edwin Mellen Press, Ltd.
Lampeter, Ceredigion, Wales
UNITED KINGDOM SA48 8LT

Printed in the United States of America

To the memory of my father

Zhengwen Gao

and to my mother

Xinping Ouyang

Table of Contents

List of Figures

List of Tables

Foreword

What your mother or father told you about lying when you were a child was probably pretty simple: Lying is not telling the truth. That's bad. Don't do it!

However, anything as culturally important as lying is bound to be more complicated. We've heard and marveled over the idea that Eskimos have many words for different kinds of snow. Actually this is a rather misleading cliché, but here let's consider the many English words and phrases for different kinds of lying. One of them is "snow job!" And there are disturbingly many others, for instance, calumny, fib, bull, dissimulation, equivocation, exaggeration, fabrication, perjury, soft-soaping, liable, whopper, and fish story, each with its own shade of meaning. No question, lying is a complicated business.

In this intriguing book, Minghui Gao reveals one face of lying in a particular and provocative cultural context, the Chinese custom of lying about good deeds. On first hearing the phrase, most of us might think: Ah, of course, people often *inappropriately claim credit* for good deeds they did not do. Surprisingly, the topic is the direct opposite of this: In China, people often *appropriately deny* good deeds they *did* do.

In Chinese culture, as in cultures around the world, truth is respected and lying despised as a general rule. However, there are nuanced exceptions such as the white lie, the polite lie, and lying about good deeds. Here, the author explores how Chinese children become enculturated to the complex ins and outs of this paradoxical practice.

The virtues of this inquiry are many. In contrast with similar studies, the approach does not rely on youngsters' reactions to imaginary scenarios, instead probing their own personal experiences of lying about good deeds or hearing others do so. The analysis examines not only whether and when children pick up on lying about good deeds but how they conceptualize what they are doing. The findings identify multiple styles of response and chart which are dominant. In revealing the intricacy of ethical and social practice around lying about good deeds, this book helps us to appreciate the subtle character of moral thought, action, and development not only within Chinese culture but beyond.

No doubt every culture has its own nuances of the lying game. Although lying about good deeds may be an especially salient characteristic of Chinese culture, as an American I'm struck by how graceful social behavior here involves something in similar spirit. One doesn't deny the good deed, but one would often say "Oh, it was nothing" or "I just happened to be there at the right time," or "Anyone would have done the same thing." Such phrases do acknowledge the deed, but they modestly deny extraordinary merit. Well, Minghui Gao would no doubt be similarly modest about the chapters to follow. But I am free to celebrate their excellence.

David Perkins
Harvard University

Acknowledgements

Many individuals have contributed in diverse ways to this book, and I would like to take this opportunity to gratefully acknowledge them. I must first acknowledge—with the deepest gratitude—David Perkins, my principal advisor through my years at Harvard University and beyond. Dave has held steady as a consistent beacon of expectation and confidence in the work that has guided me. He has advised me to chart and discover my way. Without his mentoring, my work would not have been the same.

I am also deeply grateful to Robert Selman, who has always been there to give advice and show me different ways to approach a research problem while demonstrating the need to be persistent to accomplish any goal. His provocative and responsive enthusiasm has strengthened my sense of purpose.

I wish to thank Eleanor Duckworth, who not only introduced me to her seminal teaching-research method, but also provided me with the energy, hope, and commitment that have filled the entire process of my inquiry and writing. She embodies all that I look for in an outstanding teacher and researcher.

I am also grateful to my friends. The confidence and support of Ale Blanco, Baoyan Cheng, Chunpin Han, Tao Wang, and Xu Zhao have helped sustain me through various challenges. In addition, John Murphy and John Ulrich read early drafts of this book and offered insightful suggestions. Their patience, interest, clarity, and skills provided me with the desire to strive higher.

My colleagues at Arkansas State University have been sources of intellectual enrichment and practical support through this most challenging, yet rewarding phase of my work. I wish I could name them all. I am particularly grateful to Dr. Thomas Fiala for his insightful comments on the use of many crucial concepts, Dr. James Jupp for his intellectually supportive interest in my work, and Dr. Lina Owens for her thoughtful advice on language use and the selection of cover pictures. These respectable, kind, learned, and challenging minds embody all the qualities a wonderful human being ought to have.

Finally, I owe my deepest gratitude to my wife, Hongli, whose love, encouragement, and whole-hearted assistance have nourished me on the voyage to pushing beyond the ordinary. I am also thankful for our daughters, Maggie and Melissa, who have gone through so much by missing their Daddy and seeing me work at night. Their tolerance of my absence from bedtime stories and many weekends has made it possible to immerse myself in this engulfing river of "making a book," as Maggie once called it.

Introduction

If, like truth, the lie had but one face, we would be on better terms. For we would accept as certain the opposite of what the liar would say. But the reverse of truth has a hundred thousand faces *and an infinite field.*

—Michel de Montaigne (1572/1952)

THE PHENOMENON

Lying has many forms, various justifications, and uncertain consequences. A lie can be told for personal gain, to deny responsibility, to avoid hurting someone's feelings, or simply from habit. Although lying is usually considered to be reprehensible, in certain circumstances it is encouraged. This book presents research that explores Chinese children's ethical discourse on the practice of lying about good deeds. Ethical discourse, as I use the term here, refers to "a string of statements or arguments containing 'moral statements' (statements about *what* actions or attitudes are obligatory or virtuous) and/or 'ethical statements' (statements about *why* those actions or attitudes are morally right or wrong)" (Edwards, 1985, p. 319). Lying about good deeds, in the sense of not taking credit for them, is a well-recognized behavior in Chinese society and has long been valued. Public media, for instance, are replete with stories praising sincere people who denied performing good deeds they had in fact done.

To be sure, the phrase "lying about good deeds" may jar. The Chinese do not necessarily label this phenomenon as such. Instead, they prefer such descriptive phrases as "not taking credit for doing good deeds," "doing good deeds without admitting them," and "doing good deeds without leaving one's name." Therefore, it is necessary to clarify why the present study followed the current literature (e.g., Lee, Cameron, Xu, Fu, & Board, 1997) and labeled the phenomenon as "lying about good deeds" (p. 926). To do so, I will begin with a conceptual understanding of two crucial terms, *lying* and *good deeds*. I will then exemplify the phenomenon of *lying about good deeds* using real-life stories in which individuals denied doing good deeds that they had actually committed.

The term *lying* has been conceptualized in various ways (e.g., Bok, 1979; Carson, 2006; Coleman & Kay, 1981; Kupfer, 1982; Shibles, 1985; Vrij, 2000). Just like many other elusive terms, such as *right* and *wrong*, lying has never received a universally agreed-upon definition (Mahon, 2008). Of the many factors contributing to this lack of consensus, two aspects in particular stand out. First, lying as a way of fooling people is value-laden. Countless arguments for and against lying exist in the ethical literature. Deontologists consider lying to be absolutely wrong, regardless of the consequences (Bok, 1979; Kupfer, 1982). A notable example is Immanuel Kant, who stated that under no circumstances could lying be justified (Benton, 1982). Philosophers with a more utilitarian approach, such as Desiderius Erasmus (1466/1469-1536) and Henry Sidgwick (1838-1900), believe that lying should be evaluated only by consequences and be permissible in certain situations.

In 1987, Sweetser proposed a folkloristic model of lying. For Sweetser, a spectrum of varying reprehensibility runs through different lie types. Verbal communication, including lying, is governed by culturally defined rules for social interaction. These rules operate in a hierarchy, at the top of which is the "general cooperative rule," which states that the goal of social communication is to "try to help, not to harm" (p. 47). This rule condemns harmfully motivated communicative behaviors and condones helpfully motivated communicative behaviors. Hence, an altruistically motivated lie that conforms to the general cooperative rule is considered less reprehensible than a harmfully motivated lie that violates the general cooperative rule.

Although the general cooperative rule is paramount for determining the extent to which a lie is considered to be reprehensible, the setting in which a lie occurs also contributes to people's moral judgment (Sweetser, 1987). The fundamental dimension of setting is whether a lie is told in an informational or a politeness setting. In an informational setting, the primary purpose of discourse is to convey accurate information, and discourse is expected to obey Grice's (1975) informational rule—namely, inform and do not misinform others. When a lie is told in an informational setting, it is more likely to be judged as negative (Sweetser, 1987). Meanwhile, in a politeness setting, the primary purpose of discourse is to establish and maintain positive social relations. In this setting, it is a prominent requirement that one comply with Lakoff's (1973) politeness rules—namely, do not impose but rather give options (e.g., do not demand, but ask), make others feel good, and be amicable. Hence, people will be more reluctant to judge an intentionally false statement made in a politeness setting as reprehensible.

This more moderate approach to condoning certain types of lies, even advocating their benefit for preserving social relationships, is promoted by some more recent thinkers. Nyberg (1993) exposed the tacit truth underneath our collective pretense and revealed that an occasional lie can be helpful, healthy, creative, and—in some situations—even downright moral. Nyberg stated that, without lying, it would be virtually impossible to have a relationship; society could not survive if we all felt compelled to always tell the truth. Serban (2001) argued that a person, in the process of pursuing his or her goals, tends to manipulate others. Adapting through deception, particularly in crisis, is part of our animal heritage. Our thought processes, which are protective of our emotions and self-image, are perfectly adapted for the task of lying. Serban believed that lying has played—and continues to do so—an important role in individuals' coping and survival in society.

With considerations such as these, many scholars have suggested that lying as a speech act is ambiguous in meaning. Tudor-Hart (1926) stressed the differences in motives behind deceptive statements, sorting lies into anti-social lies, social lies, and asocial lies. Chisholm and Feehan (1977) further highlighted the importance of belief in defining lying, claiming that lying is saying something that you believe to be false when you believe that your listeners are justified in believing (a) that you believe what you say and (b) that you intend them to believe that you believe what you say (p. 152). Bok (1979) defined a lie as "any intentionally deceptive message which is *stated*" (p. 14), emphasizing its intentionality and deceptiveness. Lee (2000) argued that lying could be defined in both psychological and socio-cultural terms, depending on stressing either its intentionality or conventionality. Ekman (1985) argued that concealing information with the intention to mislead another to believe something false is lying. He defined lying as follows:

> In my definition of a lie or deceit, then, one person intends to mislead another, doing so deliberately, without prior notification of this purpose, and without having been explicitly asked to do so by the target. There are two primary ways to lie: to *conceal* and to *falsify*. In concealing, the liar withholds some information without actually saying anything untrue. In falsifying, an additional step is taken. Not only does the liar withhold true information, but he presents false information as if it were true. (p. 28)

This multifaceted nature of lying as a value-laden speech act has made it difficult for scholars to arrive at consensus regarding its definition. For the purpose of the present study, I have drawn from the seminal works of Bok (1979), Chisholm and Feehan (1977), and Ekman (1985), all of whom stress the importance of intentionality, deceptiveness, and belief in defining lying. I believe that an individual is lying if he or she conceals information or provides others with a stated message that he or she does not believe with the intent that the recipient(s) of the message will believe it.

The second term to be defined for the current study is *good deeds*. Here, I use the literal translation of the Chinese concept known as *hao shi* (*hao* for good; *shi* for deed), which refers to any behaviors intended to help and not to harm others. Good deeds are also often referred to as pro-social behaviors (Lee et al., 1997). Accordingly, someone who rescues a drowning person from a freezing river has done a good deed, even if the thought of getting a medal flitted across his or her mind during the rescue. A gift to charity is a good deed even if it produces a tax deduction for the giver. A service performed by a child is a good deed even if done on assignment from his or her parents or guardians.

Some philosophers may have problems with this notion of good deeds. They may doubt whether an act is a good deed if it is done in order to be recognized or earn recognition. For them, a good deed should be a selfless act of doing something good for another with no thought of recognition and not done with the hope of a favor in return. However, if we define *good deeds* so narrowly as to exclude all acts that earn recognition, we are very likely to have a logical problem. People could argue forever about whether an act is a good deed if the doer's motives are mixed. By my understanding of the term, good deeds are likely to be recognized. The stranger to whom we give directions on the street may thank us, thus showing appreciation. Having pulled our neighbor out of the burning house, we may get a medal from the mayor a year later. Surely these acknowledgments do not knock our altruistic acts off the "good deeds" list.

Based on the above conceptualization of the terms *lying* and *good deeds*, I will concisely define *lying about good deeds* as a speech act uttered in order to conceal or provide deceptive information about one's pro-social behaviors. For example, Jianing, a fourth-grade girl, tidied up her classroom (that is, she conducted a good deed) during a class break when her classmates were not on the scene. When her teacher asked if Jianing happened to know who cleaned the room, she replied that she did not know who did it (that is, she lied). As noted earlier, Chinese people in general would label Jianing's behavior as "not taking credit for doing good deeds" rather than "lying about good deeds."

However, it is obvious that Jianing was the person who cleaned the room. When she uttered that she did not know who cleaned the room, she was providing deceptive information about her actions. Therefore, it is my understanding that Jianing was lying about a good deed that she had actually accomplished. The reality that the Chinese usually do not label Jianing's utterance as "lying" does not change to any extent the nature of her speech act as a lie, one that Jianing herself did not believe but uttered with the intent that the recipient(s) of the information would believe it.

Now, let us consider another example, from a conversation between myself (Q for Question) and Bida (A for Answer), a ninth-grade Chinese boy, over his classmate Liang's doing a good deed:

Q: Do you know anyone who has conducted good deeds?
A: Yes, I do. Last year, a student named Liang caught a thief.
Q: Really? Can you tell me something about it?
A: Sure. Liang was at that time walking in his neighborhood. He heard a notice on the neighborhood's radio that a man might have stolen a motorcycle from a family in the neighborhood. Before long, Liang noticed a young man riding on a motorcycle, so he ran up to him. When the young man noticed someone running after him, he tried to run away. Liang realized that the young man must be the suspect and thus seized him after fighting.
Q: How did you come to know about this event?
A: The Residents' Committee in Liang's neighborhood wrote our school an acknowledgement letter, which was later announced over our school radio. But I was not quite sure it was my classmate Liang who caught the thief, because several students share the same first name and surname. One day I happened to ask my classmate Liang whether it was he who conducted the deed as broadcasted. He replied very humbly that it was not him.
Q: But the truth is that he did catch the thief?

A: Yes, he was the one who caught the thief.
Q: But he told you that it was not him?
A Yeah.
Q: Was he joking?
A: No, I believe he was serious.
Q: What do you think made him deny doing the good deed?
A: Isn't there such a saying that to be an unsung hero means doing good deeds without leaving one's name? I also very much appreciate this kind of attitude. His denying the good deed seems to me to be very good.

Obviously, Liang conducted a good deed, but he replied that it was not him when his classmate Bida inquired as to whether or not it was he who had accomplished the good deed. In this sense, Liang's denial of doing the good deed falls squarely within the idea of "lying about good deeds."

However, what are we going to make of this story? What meaning would Bida, the story-teller, construct of this experience? What does it tell us about Bida's inner voice when he remarked that "[Liang's] denying the good deed seems to...be very good"? What does it reveal about Bida's ethical belief when he said he "also very much appreciate[d] this kind of attitude"? What is it that has caused Bida to appreciate being lied to by his fellow student Liang? What does it reveal about Liang's ethical thinking underlying his decision to lie about a good deed that he has in fact accomplished? If people who lie are generally motivated to escape negative consequences, to evade being negatively judged, to avoid potential embarrassment, or to prevent the target from being hurt or harmed (Tudor-Hart, 1926), why do the Chinese deny their pro-social behaviors?

EXISTING LITERATURE

This fascinating phenomenon in Chinese culture has triggered growing interest among social scientists. A fair body of literature has begun to examine

Chinese youngsters' ethical discourse on the practice of lying about good deeds. This literature evokes three themes. One theme of the literature is focused on exploring the cognitive-developmental characteristics of Chinese youngsters' categorization and evaluation of "untruthful statements" about good deeds. It is agreed that lying is ubiquitous, but attitudes toward lying vary with socio-cultural conventions (Lee, 2000). For instance, lying is automatically deplored in the American society, but there is no automatic criticism of the untruthful speech act in many contexts in China, where "moral evaluation depends on one's willingness to act appropriately in context, and one's inner state or desires are irrelevant" (Blum, 2007, p. 18). Although Chinese people generally consider honesty a virtue, they admire those who are able to conduct complex lying behaviors that require delicate planning, intelligence, cleverness, and knowledge. In contrast, dupes—while to some extent sympathized with—may be criticized for their gullibility, which often results from greed or desire. In other words, Chinese culture, while like most (if not all) cultures in the world valuing honesty, nonetheless tends to condone lying, deception, and fabrication in accordance with consequence and context (Blum, 2007, pp. 44-45).

The attitude of Chinese people toward lying is also reflected in Chinese youngsters' understanding and evaluation of untruthful statements about good deeds. In a cross-cultural study (Lee et al., 1997), 7-, 9-, and 11-year-old Chinese and Canadian children were invited to categorize and evaluate truthful and untruthful statements about good deeds. Hypothetical child story characters carried out a good deed, but they either lied or told the truth when they were questioned by a teacher as to who had conducted the deed. This study discloses several findings. First of all, in terms of categorization of lie- and truth-telling, subjects categorized story characters' truthful statements about one's good deed as "the truth" and untruthful statements about good deeds as "lies." Second, in terms of moral evaluation of untruthful statements about good deeds, Chinese children's ratings changed from negative at 7 years of age to positive at 9 and 11 years of age. Third, in terms of moral evaluation of truthful statements about good deeds, Chinese children's ratings changed with increased age. The older the children were, the less positive their ratings tended to be.

When asked why they gave negative ratings to truth-telling about good deeds, nearly half of the participants commented that the story character was "wanting" or "begging for" the teacher's praise; one third of the children stated that the story character should not admit or take credit for the good deed. In contrast, when asked why they gave positive ratings to lie-telling about good deeds, up to 90% of the children justified their evaluations by either stating that one should not leave one's name after doing a good deed (54%) or that one should not tell the teacher about the good deed (36%). In interpreting these findings, the researchers postulated that Chinese cultural emphasis on rules of right conduct such as humility or modesty might lead children, with increased acculturation, to believe that lying for the sake of conforming to the modesty rule has positive moral value, whereas truth-telling about good deeds is morally undesirable as it violates the rule of "not taking credit for doing good deeds."

In order to solidify their 1997 findings, Lee and colleagues (Lee, Xu, Fu, Cameron, & Chen, 2001) conducted another study, following the same procedure as in Lee et al. (1997) and sampling children from Taiwan (n = 90), mainland China (n = 60), and Canada (n = 60). These researchers then examined participants' categorization and evaluation of lie examples used in Lee et al. (1997). The findings of this study replicated the 1997 findings. First, in terms of conceptual understanding, children from Taiwan and mainland China categorized untruthful statements about good deeds as "lies" and truthful statements as "the truth." Second, in terms of moral evaluations of lie- and truth-telling, children from Taiwan and mainland China, as age increased, provided increasingly positive evaluations to untruthful statements about good deeds while giving less and less positive ratings to truthful statements about good deeds. Third, in terms of age group, 7-year-olds from Taiwan and mainland China tended to give negative ratings to lying about good deeds while 9-year-olds' ratings tended to be near neutral or balanced; however, 11-year-olds tended to give positive ratings.

What's more, of the 7-year-olds who gave negative ratings to lying about good deeds, approximately 40% justified their negative ratings by accusing the story character of "lying" or being "dishonest." Of the 9-year-olds who gave neutral or balanced ratings to lying about good deeds, more than 70% cited the balance between lying and good deeds to justify their ratings, and more than one quarter also used modesty-related justifications. Of the 11-year-olds who gave positive ratings to lying about good deeds, more than 80% offered modesty-related justifications, commenting that the story character "does not want others to know his/her good deed," "is not bragging," "does not seek praise," "has humility," "is telling a well intentioned lie," and "is modest." As evidenced in this study, Chinese youngsters' ethical reasoning takes the form of conforming to rules—from honesty at 7 years of age to modesty at 11 years of age. According to the interpretation of Lee et al. (2001), Chinese cultural emphasis on conforming to rules such as modesty contributes to Chinese children's increasing positive attitudes toward lying about good deeds.

To extend Lee et al.'s (1997, 2001) findings, Fu, Lee, Cameron, and Xu (2001) also conducted a cross-cultural study to determine how Chinese and Canadian college students categorize and evaluate lie- and truth-telling about good deeds. Presented with the same hypothetical stories as used by Lee et al. (1997, 2001), participants were asked to categorize and evaluate untruthful statements told about pro-social deeds. Overall, Chinese college students were less inclined to label an untruthful statement made in the pro-social situation as "a lie" than Canadians, but both groups labeled a truthful statement in the pro-social situation as "the truth." Specifically, 45% of Chinese college students did not categorize untruthful statements about good deeds as "lies," whereas more than 80% of Canadian students labeled such statements as lies. In contrast, with a few exceptions, 95% of the Chinese students, like their Canadian counterparts (100%), categorized truthful statements about good deeds as the "truth."

Furthermore, approximately 50% of the Chinese college students labeled untruthful statements about good deeds as "lies," but rated lying about good deeds positively; the other half of the Chinese college students did not categorize untruthful statements about good deeds as "lies" and gave even more positive ratings to the untruthful statements. However, the ratings of the Chinese students who categorized untruthful statements about good deeds as "lies" were significantly less positive than those of the Chinese students who labeled untruthful statements about good deeds as "not lies." The researchers asserted that lying about good deeds has to do with the Chinese cultural emphasis on the "humility" or "modesty" rule, arguing that emphasis on humility plays an important role in shaping youngsters' understanding and evaluation of lying about good deeds.

Another theme of the existing literature (e.g., Bond, Leung, & Wan, 1982; Davin, 1991; Price, 1992) is featured by documenting the socialization of Chinese children to socio-cultural rules (e.g., modesty, sense of shame) related to reporting good deeds. One central observation is that, in Chinese society, children's socialization to rules of right conduct in the area of modesty or humility is consciously used to produce an adult person who is humble and modest, one who is "good" in the eyes of others (Wang, 2004). Chinese schools at all levels are required to foster students' awareness of personal humility or modesty, and students are expected to act with modesty in both behavioral conduct and in academic achievement (Davin, 1991). In the Chinese school curriculum, modesty is strongly emphasized and is a central criterion whereby children's school comportment is assessed (Price, 1992). In addition, Chinese parents instruct their children to be modest and avoid self-aggrandizement or bragging about personal achievements, including high marks and good deeds, so as to avoid negative social evaluations.

It is generally believed that a person who violates the rule of modesty and brags about personal achievements or good deeds is to be regarded as one who has no sense of shame and has to face very negative social evaluation as Chinese culture, along with other Asian cultures, has long been characterized as a "shame culture" (Benedict, 1946). Chinese people regard sense of shame as "the bottom line" for a human being; to put it in Mencius's words, "Whoever has no sense of shame is not human" (Yang, 1960, p. 80, cited in Wang, 2004). It is believed that unless one has a sense of shame, he or she would do things that offend public decency. Therefore, it is critical to foster in a person an awareness of sense of shame and a feeling of disgrace or "a sense of self-blame brought on by the condemnation of others" (Wang, 2004, p. 438). As part of the endeavor to promote one's sense of shame, both self-effacement and modesty are directly encouraged (Bond et al., 1982).

Still another theme evident in the existing studies is characterized by conceptual speculation on the socio-moral nature of lying about good deeds. In his 2000 book *The exemplary society: Human improvement, social control, and the dangers of modernity in China*, Bakken explored the nature of lying about good deeds. He postulated that Chinese people practice lying about good deeds not because they do not want their good deeds to be known by others but because they conform to the Chinese socio-moral norm of "doing the right thing" (e.g., lying about good deeds) to be perceived as "good" by others. Bakken observed that Chinese society "explicitly stresses the importance of surface behavior as the 'outward sign of human civilization' and the 'external manifestation (*waizai biaoxian*) of human relations'" (p. 416); therefore, *biaoxian* (performance) may be the best expression that can explain "the acting character and falseness of the Chinese" (p. 419).

According to Bakken's (2000) observation, in learning pro-social behavior, "the stress is on biaoxian" (*zhongzai biaoxian*) and Chinese people from schooldays are modeled to be "actors…who pretend to be good persons" (p. 419).

Bakken realizes that it would be ethno-centric for a Westerner to accuse the Chinese of "hypocrisy" because the Greco-Western roots of truth and falsity do not apply to China (p. 416). Nonetheless, Bakken maintains that one could not help noting that lying about good deeds is simply a type of "performance" the Chinese put on in a specific social context (p. 414) or "simulation" whereby one pretends to be someone one is actually not (p. 422). Thus, according to Bakken, individuals who do not take credit for their good deeds are in essence "other-ruled" social actors.

As we can see, existing literature expands to some degree our knowledge about and understanding of lying about good deeds. It reveals the cognitive-developmental characteristics of Chinese youngsters' understanding and evaluation of lying about good deeds. It also discloses the age patterns of youngsters' rule orientation. For 7-year-olds, honesty takes precedence over modesty; thus, not telling the truth about one's good deed violates the rule "honesty" and is morally wrong. In addition, the current literature discloses to some extent the way in which the Chinese are socialized to conform to the norm of "doing the right thing to become good in the eyes of others."

These studies of lie- and truth-telling about good deeds appear to be limited in at least two major aspects. One limitation is their interpretative perspective. Studies to date—almost without exception—rely upon the "rule justification" to interpret the socio-psychological dynamics of Chinese youngsters' ethical discourse on lying about good deeds. They postulate that Chinese individuals' practical behaviors and evaluative decisions of lying about good deeds are associated with their conformity to social-cultural rules, such as modesty and performance (*biaoxian*). This rule (or rule-governed) justification surely discloses an important dimension of the psychology of lying about good deeds. However, this one-dimensional interpretative perspective is certainly not adequate to unpack the rationale underlying a complex area such as lying about good deeds. I believe that other dimensions may exist for which the current literature does not account.

The other limitation of the current literature is its inquiry approach. Existing studies are characterized by "a strictly cognitive, formal (that is, abstract), and hypothetical focus of cognitive-developmental approach" (Tappan, 1991, p. 245). They seek to link individuals' practical behaviors (namely, not telling the truth about one's good deeds) to their moral beliefs (namely, conforming to socio-cultural rules such as humility or performance) without considering the "mental steps leading to the expression of intended action" (Sigel, 1985, p. 346). They rarely take into consideration individuals' lived experiences around lying about good deeds in real-life settings and their meaning-making of various attitudes and practices around lying about good deeds. In other words, studies to date have relied on contrived hypothetical settings to elicit participants' categorizations and evaluations of story characters' practice of lying about good deeds. The data collected reflect the subjects' empathic capacity more than the full-rounded self-context in which moral decisions are made.

According to Saltzstein (1994), both moral judgment and moral behavior are moral decisions; moral judgment is an evaluative decision, while moral behavior is a behavioral decision. Moral judgment or evaluation as decision-making is characterized by a self-vs.-other discrepancy; moral decisions made from the self's perspective differ from decisions made from an observer's perspective (Saltzstein, 1994; Turiel & Wainryb, 1993). Specifically, people judge and evaluate their own actions taking into account not only the well-being of the recipient of the actions but also their own well-being, self-interest, consequences, and emotional experiences. In contrast, when people judge and evaluate others' actions, they take a rule-governed orientation and use as criteria the moral rules or principles others' actions conform to or violate.

This self-vs.-other discrepancy is evidenced in a pilot study I conducted to explore Chinese children's ethical reasoning about the rightness or obligation of lying about good deeds. The results of the pilot study indicated that Chinese children who judged story characters' lie-telling about good deeds as morally wrong justified their judgment by consistently commenting that the story characters were dishonest or they should be honest. When the same Chinese children were asked whether they would tell the truth about the good deed if they were the story characters, more than half of them answered that they would not tell the truth. They justified their decisions by referring to either the attitude of their teachers (authorities), peers' skepticism (social consequences), embarrassment (personal feelings), or humility (socio-cultural rules). This finding is consistent with Aiken's (1952) deliberation, inspired by British philosopher David Hume (1711-1776):

> The interests which support "morality" are many. Custom, habit, sympathy, fear, the love of reputation, and a thousand other motives, together with the myriadic non-moral "reasons" that reinforce them, combine to secure moral action upon a far more solid base than would be possible were we to rely exclusively on moral justifications. (p. 242)

It seems that overcoming the second limitation, by taking a different inquiry approach, might help overcome the limitation inherent in the interpretative perspective. Therefore, I want to present a more robust picture of Chinese children's ethical discourse on lying about good deeds by taking a narrative approach and inviting the participants to revisit their own lived moral experiences.

A NARRATIVE APPROACH

The term *narrative* derives from the Latin verb *narrare*, which means "to recount" or "to tell about." Narrative is a form in which discrete activities and events are described as having a meaningful and coherent order, creating a unity or meaningfulness that reality does not inherently possess. Narrative, as "a particular genre" of discourse, is a primary mode by which meaning—particularly moral meaning—is ascribed to sequential or discursive activities and events (Tappan, 1991, p. 245; White, 1981). Narrative forms exist in the recollection of life events, in historical documents, in political speeches, and in day-to-day conversations (Nash, 1994, p. xi). Life experience gives rise to and forms narratives and at the same time is itself given meaning in the dynamic process of narrating and listening.

Narratives are made up not only of actions and events but also of characters or personages; a narrative unites all the elements that are contingencies (Ricoeur, 1990/1992). An individual's experience usually consists of disparate and somehow discordant elements; narratives help draw together these elements into the concordant unity of a story. Thus, a narrative tells of not only the connections that unify multiple actions and events over a span of time performed, in most cases, by a multiplicity of characters but also the connections that link multiple viewpoints on and assessments of those actions and events. A narrative eventually becomes one whereby the individual identity of one personage intersects those of others. In this intersection emerge second-order stories (e.g., stories about relationships and families) that tell about the intertwining of multiple individual stories.

Therefore, narratives provide a means for researchers to examine the meanings people—whether individually or collectively—ascribe to lived experiences (Eastmond, 2007, p. 248). They create a uniquely powerful vehicle for understanding human experience, especially human moral experience (MacIntyre, 1981). They provide access to personal and cultural values to which we otherwise have little access (Bortolussi & Dixon, 2003). In other words, narratives can be instrumental in helping us gain knowledge about how individuals acquire, organize, and make meanings of lived experience (Potter &

Wetherell, 1987; Lamarque, 1990); how they shape their experience of reality (White, 1981; Ricoeur, 1983); and how they are affected by cultural codes and norms (Bortolussi & Dixon, 2003).

Narrative approaches used in much of today's qualitative research are in essence grounded in a phenomenological assumption (Eastmond, 2007). Specifically, phenomenology assumes that individuals ascribe meaning to phenomena which they experience and that one can only know something about others' experiences from the expressions they give them (Schutz, 1972, pp. 99-100). Phenomenology "aims to identify and describe the subjective experience of respondents. It is a matter of studying everyday experience from the point of view of the subject, and shuns critical evaluation of forms of social life" (Schwandt, 2001, p. 192). In short, it seeks to understand an event or experience from the point of view of the experiencing subject.

Understandably, narrative approaches have been relied upon as the means for researchers to "[know] something about life in times and places to which we have little other access" and "about how people themselves, as 'experiencing subjects,' make sense" of attitudes and practices in the domain of social transaction (Eastmond, 2007, p. 249). As a result, narrative approaches, such as life histories and personal narratives, have long been employed in a wide range of scholarly fields to fulfill various theoretical orientations and research interests, such as history, cultural and developmental psychology, and anthropology.

The early 1980s witnessed growing interest among researchers in narrative approaches to explore lived experience and the subjective dimension of social life (Eastmond, 2007, p. 248). The field of moral development—once dominant within the social learning paradigm and the cognitive-developmental approach, as suggested by Wilson (1981)—now also caught the eye of those engaged in applying narrative approaches to recounting moral actions and events of experiencing subjects (Eastmond, 2007). Inspired in large measure by the ground-breaking works of Carol Gilligan and her colleagues (Gilligan, 1977, 1982;

Gilligan & Attanucci, 1988; Tappan, 1989, 1990, 1991; Tappan & Packer, 1991), narrative was found to provide a means of "[listening] to individuals' stories of real-life moral conflict and choice"; the turn toward narrative approaches provided "an important corrective" in the study of moral development (Tappan, 1991, p. 244).

All narratives have ethical dimensions. They present characters in such a way that evaluations of what they do or suffer are ingredients in the very meaning of the recounted actions or events of the experiencing subjects (Ricoeur, 1990/1992). In fact, narratives have been understood by philosophers as "an indispensable laboratory for the exemplification of ethical questions" (Erll, 2009). Aristotle believed that ethos was a key component of rhetoric. Modern philosophers, such as Michel Foucault, Hans-Georg Gadamer, Alasdair MacIntyre, and Richard Rorty, have all contributed to the "long and influential tradition of philosophical thinking about the inherently ethical dimension of narrative" (Erll, 2009)

Foucault (1997), for instance, argued that ethics has to do with the kind of relationship one ought to have with oneself and determines how one is supposed to constitute oneself as a moral subject of one's own actions (p. 263). The constitution of the self as a moral subject, according to Foucault (1978), involves searching out four major aspects: ethical substance, mode of subjectivation, *techne* of the self, and *telos* of action. The ethical substance is our feelings, which is "the prime material of moral conduct." The mode of subjectivation is "the way in which [the] individual establishes his relation to the rule and recognizes himself as obligated to put it into practice." The *techne* of the self is the self-forming activity—that is, the means or practices by which we can change ourselves in order to become ethical subjects. Finally, the *telos* of action is the kind of being to which we aspire when we behave in a moral way (Foucault, 1978, pp. 26-27).

According to Foucault (1978), our selves are always formed in activities in which recommended practices are available as discourse. The aspect of the self concerned with moral conduct and the source of our obligation function together to support the means or practices by which one forms the self. In other words, the means or practices we might take in order to form the self become occasions in which we construct the insight that guides our actions toward a moral being. Ethics, therefore, is not a body of rules or prescriptions for right conduct, but a self-forming activity guided by recommended practices (p. 27).

Like all lived experiences, self-forming activities in which our moral being is constituted exist in time, space, and relationships and therefore require us to consider and appreciate the multi-faceted character of the discourse through which human moral lives are realized (Gilligan, Brown, & Rogers, 1990; Moore, 1987; Tappan, 1989, 1991; Tappan & Packer, 1991). Stories are told in situations shaped through the dynamic interplay and power relationship between narrator and listener (Crapanzano, 1980; Gadamer, 1975; Skultans, 1999). If we are to see the power relations embedded in any system of knowledge, we need to take into account the present as well as the imagined future in revisiting and interpreting the past; and we need to examine the self-forming activities or discourses in which we are embedded (Moore, 1987, p. 82).

The experience of lying about good deeds, as well as telling the story of the experience, has multiple meanings that contribute to the child's developing moral self. Due to the complexity of the relationship between experience and expressions, the analysis of the child's self-forming activities or experience is expected to distinguish at least four levels: (a) *life as lived*: the sequential or discursive events that have to do with one's life; (b) *life as experienced*: how one perceives and ascribes meaning to what happens, drawing on previous experience, cultural repertoires, and recommended practices; (c) *life as told*: how experience is framed and articulated in a particular context and to a particular audience; and (d) *life as text*: the researcher's interpretation and representation of the story (Bruner, 1986; Eastmond, 2007; Gadamer, 1975).

Within the narrative literature, research is seen as involving representation of "the multiple constructions that various respondents have made" in the form of words, phrases, or other meaningful units contained in respondents' narratives (Lincoln & Guba, 1985, p. 212). A narrative researcher construes events differently as a result of having encountered different experiences (Kelly, 1955) as experience is never directly represented, but edited at different stages of the process from life to text. The nature of the inquiry as well as the personal experience and cultural assumptions of the researcher are all filters through which the story is sifted and represented as text. Therefore, a narrative researcher needs to describe "the range of experience rather than the average experience" through prolonged engagement (Krefting, 1991, p. 216).

As representation—rather than documentation—of reality, narratives become methodologically complex while also opening up theoretically interesting possibilities. First, narratives make room for a dynamic view of the individual as a subject acting in the world and reflecting on actions. As such, narratives also provide an opportunity or entry point from which to grasp the interplay between self and society, letting us see the "subjective mapping of experience, the working out of a culture, and a social system" often obscured in typifying accounts (Behar, 1990, p. 225). Finally, narratives can tell us something about how social actors make sense of their world from a particular social position and cultural vantage point. Culture is thus central to both the lived experience and narrative, not only in the making of a meaningful story by a particular subject, but also in the ways in which others understand and retell that story. Therefore, for the purpose of the present study, I adopted a narrative approach to examine Chinese children's ethical discourse as expressed and represented in their stories of lying about good deeds.

Anchored in the narrative approach, this study was guided by the main research question: What are the features of Chinese children's ethical discourse as expressed and represented in their narratives of lying about good deeds in real-life settings? To answer this main research question, this inquiry specifically focused on unpacking the following questions: (a) How do Chinese children describe their experiences related to lying (or truth-telling) about good deeds? (b) What meanings do they actually construct of various attitudes and practices of lying about good deeds? (c) How do Chinese children evaluate and justify the attitudes and practices of lying or truth-telling in real-life situations involving good deeds? (d) What are the patterns featuring their ethical discourse on lying about good deeds?

CHAPTER 1
Conceptual Framework

There are occasions in every life in which one must take a stand, or make a decision to act one way rather than another. Yet the question is always present concerning the problem of which insight should guide action.

—Mary Candace Moore (1987)

ETHICAL DISCOURSE

The term *discourse*, according to Johnson (2005), originated in the field of linguistics, initially referring to whole units of speech (conversations) and the speech community in which units are communicated. Foucault (1972) transformed the concept of discourse from its linguistic formulation and applied it to the social sciences, emphasizing that discourses affect everything in our society while remaining nearly unobservable. As an institutionalized way of speaking, a discourse provides a unified set of words, symbols, and metaphors that allow us to construct and communicate a coherent interpretation of reality. It determines not only what we say and how we say it, but also what we do not say. In addition to its effects on our rhetoric, a discourse determines what entities are constructed, which relationships are considered natural, and who has agency within the discourse. Overall, discourse creates the pre-debate consensus that will affect how the rest of the debate will proceed.

Certainly, moral discourse, "the language by whose means we communicate to each other and state for ourselves our moral convictions and doubts" (Edwards, 1955, p. 19), is very manifold. Certain words occur in such contexts with great frequency—especially the words *good* and *evil*, *desirable* and *undesirable*, *right* and *wrong*, and *duty*, *ought*, and *obligation*. These terms, according to the widespread practice among philosophers and particularly moral philosophers, are referred to as "moral" predicates (Edwards, 1955, p. 19). They in fact prescribe much of our argumentation concerning moral beliefs and values.

In order to reveal the full depth of meaning and breadth of application, Aiken (1952) posited that moral discourse contained four distinctive levels: expressive, moral, ethical, and post-ethical. For Aiken, ethical discourse is the discourse level upon which we are occasionally obliged to ask whether an action that we agree is prescribed by existing moral rules is really right and thus whether we ought to continue to obey such rules. According to Aiken, the most distinctive feature of ethical discourse is its so-called autonomy. It makes no promises of future benefit to the individual who holds to a certain mode of ethical discourse; nor are its principles justified by an ulterior consideration of expediency.

Gustafson (1990; see also Curran, 2005) classified moral discourse into four types: ethical, prophetic, narrative, and policy discourse. For Gustafson, ethical discourse determines how we ought to act in particular circumstances as well as justify our particular action or non-action (p. 129). He argued that ethical discourse centers on "the use of concepts, distinctions, and modes of discourse formulated over centuries in the disciplines of moral philosophy and moral theology" (p. 127). The proper attitude of ethical discourse includes "our emotions, affective responses, and as well perceptions that cannot be reduced to data and concepts appropriate to ethical discourse" (p. 131). In short, ethical discourse provides arguments (p. 137).

Edwards (1985), as previously noted, believed that ethical discourse refers to "a string of statements or arguments containing 'moral statements' (statements about *what* actions or attitudes are obligatory or virtuous) and/or 'ethical statements' (statements about *why* those actions or attitudes are morally right or wrong)" (p. 319). For Edwards, aspects of ethical discourse can be validly abstracted from their cultural context, and "human beings from different cultural traditions can quite easily understand one another's ethical discourse" (p. 336). She concludes that ethical discourse in various cultural communities in fact "draws from a common human pool of modes of judging, choosing, justifying, and validating moral action" (p. 336).

The works of theorists such as Aiken, Edwards, and Gustafson appear to resonate with each other in terms of their definitional understandings of ethical discourse. These theorists not only illustrate to some extent the descriptive and evaluative character of ethical discourse, in the terms proposed by Chipman (1971), but also contribute to our initial understanding of the effects that ethical discourse has on our moral actions and justifications. Nonetheless, they do not illustrate how ethical discourse as a construct can be analyzed empirically. For instance, what are the modes—if any—of ethical discourse? How can we distinguish one mode from another? What are the elements featuring a certain mode of ethical discourse? With these questions in mind, I started looking for an operational framework that might help me conceptualize and analyze Chinese children's ethical discourse. After a close examination of Tipton's (1982, 2002) typology of American ethical discourse, I realized that Tipton's paradigm is theoretically informative and analytically user-friendly, thereby providing a suggestive model for the present study.

TIPTON'S TYPOLOGY

Human action, according to Parsons's (1961) "General Theory of Action," must be understood in conjunction with the motivational component, such as ends, purpose, and ideals, of the act. Parsons criticized attempts to reduce human life to psychological, biological, or materialist forces. Based on Parsons's "General Theory of Action," Potter (1965) examined American ethical evaluations around the policy of the United States regarding the possession and use of nuclear weapons. Potter's analysis revealed that American expression of ethical evaluations was characteristic of four distinctive styles: revelational-authoritative, regular, situational, and teleological (p. 369). Behind each style is a distinctive pattern of ethical reasoning.

According to Potter (1965), the revelational-authoritative style holds that a human action is illegitimate if it does not conform to the revealed will of God or legitimate if preceded by the struggle of the people of God to uphold His order and justice (p. 370). For the regular style, a human action is illegitimate if it violates certain reasonable rules of right conduct or legitimate if it provides for the military-political implementation of ethical principles. The situational style holds that a human action is illegitimate if in light of our responsibilities within the total situation it is unfitting and obnoxious to good moral sense but legitimate if in light of our responsibilities within the total situation it may be seen to be fitting and appropriate. Finally, for the teleological style, a human action is illegitimate if it will result in disastrous consequences or legitimate if it is the necessary means of obtaining a state of affairs considered desirable by the relative consensus of opinion.

Based on Potter's four-factor conceptual paradigm, Tipton (1982, 2002) advanced a conceptual framework for the analysis of ethical discourse. In his 1982 book *Getting saved from sixties: Moral meaning in conversion and cultural change*, Tipton illustrated that these four ideal styles of ethical discourse—namely, the authoritative style, the regular style, the consequential style, and the expressive style—were flourishing in American society. Tipton also found that the defining characteristics of each style could be revealed by attending to several dimensions, such as general ethical orientation, form of discourse, and right-making characteristics.

The authoritative style of ethical discourse in American society (Tipton, 1982, pp. 3-5) is embodied in "the revelation form of biblical morality." This style is mainly characterized by a strong ethical orientation toward an authoritative moral source (e.g., God) known by faith. In terms of its form of discourse, the authoritative style poses the moral question "What should I do?" in the form "What does God command?" and answers it by specifying an act that is "obedient" and "faithful." Regarding the issue of what makes a right action, the authoritative style holds to a deontological theory; in other words, apart from its predictable consequences, an act is considered right and obligatory in itself because the authoritative source commands it, and obedience to moral authority is the very virtue of a person and makes him or her most worthy of praise. For the authoritative style, moral disagreement is resolved by a "literal exegesis of scripture" and increased familiarity with it and ultimately by conversion. The authoritative style yields the greatest possible prescription of particular acts by means of commandments and regulations that can be casuistically applied to particular cases.

The regular style (Tipton, 1982, pp. 5-6) is embodied in "the rationalist line of development in biblical morality." It is mainly oriented toward rules or principles of right conduct as discerned by reason. The regular style poses the moral question "What should I do?" in the form "What is the relevant rule or principle?" and answers it by specifying an act that is "right" or "obligatory" according to the rules. The regular style also holds to a deontological theory of right action: An act is right not only by virtue of its consequences, but also because it conforms in itself to relevant rules and principles. Rationality in discerning and enacting moral principles is the very virtue of a person and makes him or her most worthy of praise. The regular style resolves moral disagreement by reasoning dialectically (from problem to solution to generalized, consistent principles to other problems) to increasingly abstract principles consistently generalizable to the most cases.

The consequential style (Tipton, 1982, pp. 6-14) is embodied in "utilitarian individualism." This style is featured with a strong ethical orientation toward "the wants of agents" and tends to determine what is good and which act is right in virtue of cost-benefit calculations. The consequential style poses the moral question "What should I do?" in the form "What do I want? What act will most satisfy it?" and answers it by specifying an act that is most "efficient" or "effective" in producing the consequences that satisfy a given want. The consequential style holds to a teleological theory of right action: An act is right because it maximizes wanted consequences. Efficiency in maximizing one's wants makes one most worthy of praise. The consequential style resolves moral disagreement by referring to the pertinent empirical evidence and ultimately by a "social-scientific explanation of alternative perceptions of the facts."

Finally, the expressive style (Tipton, 1982, pp. 14-20) is embodied in the American counterculture that emerged in the 1960s. This ethical discourse style suggests a strong ethical orientation toward "the quality of personal feelings and of situations known by intuition." For the expressive style, the moral question "What should I do?" is best represented in the discourse form "What's happening?" and answered with an act that is most "fitting" in response. The right-making theory of the expressive style holds that an act is right "because it constitutes the most fitting response to the situation and the most appropriate or honest expression of one's self." One's "sensitivity of feeling and situational response" makes a person most worthy of praise. The expressive style resolves moral disagreement by "exchanging discrepant intuitions within the context of ongoing social interaction, thereby reshaping the situation (or community), and the agent's consciousness as formed as the situation."

Overall, Tipton's typology of ethical discourse is not only highly differentiated, but also systematically integrated, thereby providing a suggestive model for the present study. I did not turn to Tipton's paradigm until I had already coded part of my data and identified four initial themes featuring Chinese children's ethical discourse. After close examination, I found that Tipton's (1982) typology of ethical discourse not only fit well with my initial thematization, but would also help solidify my initial coding and thematizing. However, I did not make use of every category of Tipton's paradigm. This decision stemmed from two major considerations.

On the one hand, Tipton's typology of ethical discourse was concretely grounded in American biblical religion, utilitarian individualism, and the counterculture that emerged in the 1960s. It in large measure reflected the way in which Americans who, consciously or unconsciously, joined these movements made moral sense of the society and their own lives within it. Undoubtedly, Tipton's paradigm provides a useful model for the analysis of American ethical discourse (Sanders, 1991). However, it is agreed that differences exist between American culture and Chinese culture. The United States is generally considered an individualistic, low-context society, at the core of which is the belief in the freedom of the individual (Rosenberg, 2004). Within this society, individual rights supersede "blind duty" to one's family, clan, ethnic group, or nation, and it is individual, personal guilt that serves as "a moral compass" (Cohen, 1997; see also Rosenberg, 2004). In contrast, China is generally considered a collectivistic, or interdependent, high-context society. Quite often, this high-context society is characteristically a hierarchical and traditional culture, in which group honor and harmony are of utmost importance. In an interdependent society, the concepts of shame and honor are much more important than they are in low-context, individualized societies; being humiliated or losing face before the group can be a fate worse than death in some cases (Cohen, 1997, p. 133).

On the other hand, Tipton's four ideal styles of American ethical discourse seem to be in large measure independent from—or even exclusive to—one another. One style would hardly lead people to reason or behave as other styles do, as each of them is embodied in highly exclusive religious or cultural movements and seems to exclude the possible validity of other styles. In contrast, Chinese ethical discourse is fundamentally shaped by Chinese philosophic traditions, such as Confucianism, Taoism, and Buddhism.[1] These traditions in combination form "the backbone of the Chinese culture" (Lu, 2001, p. 410) and have been synthesized as a holistic entity that promotes a good life. As Lu (2001) so elegantly put it, Chinese people "may act in accordance with Confucianism when they are interacting with other people, with Taoism when they are faced with nature, and with Buddhism when they are confronted with themselves." As such, it is no longer necessary or possible to differentiate them "in [the] mundane life of the mass[es]" (p. 412). To put it another way, the styles of Chinese ethical discourse, while each entailing defining features, are expected to some extent to be interconnected as a holistic entity (Wang, 2008). The narratives of an individual may entail the characteristics of one predominant discourse style while simultaneously recognizing the possible validity of other styles.

CHINESE SOCIO-MORAL CULTURE

Shared knowledge, beliefs, and assumptions play a critical role in interpersonal communication and in interpreting meanings of text (Kaplan & Green, 1995). Chinese children's ethical discourse is fundamentally rooted in the Chinese socio-moral context. The present study attempts to disclose the features of Chinese children's ethical discourse on the practice of lying about good deeds. Thus, it is necessary to discuss the relevant aspects of Chinese socio-moral culture in which Chinese children's ethical discourse is grounded. Characteristics such as strong obedience to authority, conformism to socio-moral rules of right conduct, emphasis on harmonious interpersonal interactions, and a growing tendency toward emotional expressions all function together and help shape Chinese character and behavior.

---

[1] Buddhism is not an indigenous Chinese tradition, but was brought to China by Buddhist monks from India during the latter part of the Han dynasty (206 B.C.–220 A.D.). It took over a century for Buddhism to become assimilated into Chinese culture.

Obedience to Authority

Chinese socio-moral culture is deeply rooted in a system of hierarchical authority advocated by Confucian ethics and characterized by a strong sensitivity toward and even dependence on the attitudes and/or responses of family, social, and political authority. The system of hierarchical authority dates back to the ancient Chinese society, which was characterized by "a dual existence," with the social elite presiding at the top of the societal pyramid and the vast majority of working people ruled at the bottom (Lu, 2001). The social elite's ideals were recorded and carried down through the writings and teachings of various philosophical traditions, such as Confucianism, Legalism, Mohism, Taoism, and Buddhism (Bond & Hwang, 1986).

For scholars, these philosophical traditions may be entirely different from and even contradictory to each other; however, for the ordinary people, they have been synthesized, reinterpreted, and utilized to promote a good life. It is no longer possible to differentiate in any thorough way the present-day manifestations of these traditions in Chinese moral character. Nevertheless, Confucianism, serving as a system of ethics, has undeniably profoundly shaped the mentality of Chinese people and "guides the behavior of most Chinese" (Ma, 1988, p. 202); indeed, "all Chinese people [are] enmeshed in the Confucian tradition" (Bond & Hwang, 1986, p. 215). Thus, Confucianism has inevitably commanded the center stage in most of the theories advanced to explain and predict Chinese character and behavior (Bond & Hwang, 1986).

Confucius (551–479 B.C.), the first Chinese philosopher who formulated an "earth-bound thought system" (Lu, 2001, p. 410), lived during a time of socio-political instability and often moved in and out of political appointments. These experiences impinged directly on the formation of Confucius's foremost ideal of social harmony, the most treasured social value of his time and beyond (Bodde, 1953, cited in Bond & Hwang, 1986). Confucius emphasized that, for the sake of social harmony, each agent should act strictly in accordance with his or her role requirements designated by a system of hierarchical authority.

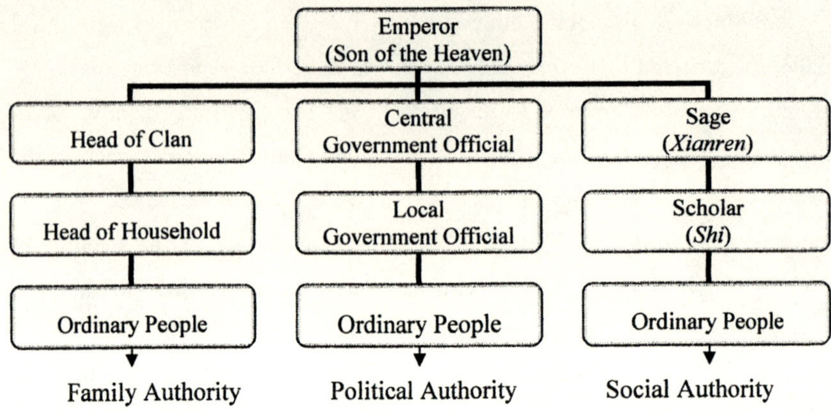

Figure 1. The System of Hierarchical Authority in Ancient China. Adapted from Wen (2005, pp. 44-46)

This system, as illustrated in Figure 1, consists of family, social, and political authority, with the emperor presiding at the top of them (Wen, 2005). Chinese attitudes toward authority, according to Perkins (1999), are characterized by dependence, acceptance, and submission. Specifically, in traditional Chinese family, youngsters are dependent upon elders and must be absolutely obedient to elders. In Chinese social life, "there is a great tendency of permanent acceptance of one's position in the social structure; and in government, administration is traditionally carried out through a sophisticated bureaucracy" (Perkins, 1999, p. 241).

The essence of Confucianism is the system of hierarchical authority (Solomon, 1971), at the heart of which is the Five-Cardinal Relations (*wulun*) initiated by Confucius and elucidated by Mencius (370–286 B.C.), a great Confucian thinker (Zhu, 1992). The five relations are those between the sovereign and subject, father and son, elder brother and younger brother, husband and wife, and friend and friend. These relationships, even those between friends, were constructed in hierarchical patterns (Fairbank, 1966). In each of the Five-Cardinal Relations, the senior member was given a wide range of prerogatives and authority with respect to the junior (Bond & Hwang, 1986, p. 215).

Since gaining predominance during the Han Dynasty (206 B.C.–220 A.D.), the Confucian system of hierarchical authority has been espoused and exercised by rulers throughout Chinese history. It should be pointed out that this system was originally in large measure a conceptual ideal. It was Tung Chung-Shu (179–104 B.C.) who converted these concepts into a practical system of values, and Chu Hsi (1130–1200) who recast these values into powerful criteria of moral behavior for the entire society (Wen, 2005). The Chinese accepted the hierarchical structure of society and developed their obedience to family, social, and political authority. For them, people at lower ranks must obey those at higher ranks without qualification (Wen, 2005).

The authoritative orientation in Chinese socio-moral culture is well evidenced in the empirical literature. Lassiter (1998) observed that Chinese people "demonstrated great respect for their elderly, based not only on recognition of their elder's experience, technical knowledge, and property ownership...but mainly on the Confucian philosophy of reverence for age" (p. 72). Chu (1967) documented that Chinese character and social behavior are characterized by submission to authority. Cross-cultural studies in communication styles (e.g., Wang & Leichtman, 2000) have found that the Chinese, including the westernized Hong Kong Chinese, have a strong authoritative orientation; in both private and public settings, they try to avoid questioning the ideas of authority figures (e.g., professors, teachers), avoid conflicts with authority figures, and show respect to and save "face" for authority figures.

Yu and Wen (2004) reported that a strong authoritative orientation exists in Chinese, especially mainland Chinese, "reported speech" of authoritative sources. When quoting authority figures (e.g., Confucius), the Chinese tend to repeat the words or scriptures of an authoritative source without any modification or reinterpretation. Wilson also conducted a series of studies in Chinese moral development and political socialization (Wilson 1970, 1974, 1981). In his cross-cultural studies focused on youngsters' attitudes toward authority, Wilson (1981) documented a strong authoritative orientation among Chinese children. When asked (a) whether one should openly argue with an authority figure and (b) whether one should question an authority figure, the majority of Chinese children in Taiwan (83% and 100%, respectively), Hong Kong (78% and 67%, respectively), and New York Chinatown (67% and 50%, respectively) negatively responded to both questions. In contrast, only 17% and 33% of European American children in New Jersey offered the same answers.

As can be seen, Chinese socio-moral culture entails a strong authoritative orientation that is shaped by the system of hierarchical authority and characterized by sensitivity to the presence, response, and instruction of family, social, and political authority. Just as Hsu (1948) pointed out, one important facet of the Chinese culture is the deference and respect shown to persons high in social or occupational status (see also Huang & Harris, 1973). Chinese people have a strong sense of dependence upon the attitudes and/or responses of authority figures; for them, political leaders, scholars or teachers, and parents or grandparents are the immediate authoritative moral sources to which they are obedient and upon which they are dependent when facing moral dilemmas. They tend to judge the goodness and obligation of an act in accordance with the attitude, response, or instructions of authority figures. For many Chinese people, the attitudes and/or responses of authority figures would be the justifications for rightness or wrongness of an act; sensitivity or obedience to the requirements, instructions, or orders of authority figures would be that which makes a person most worthy of praise in private and public settings.

CONFORMISM TO SOCIO-MORAL RULES

Chinese socio-moral culture is also characterized by strong conformism to *li* and oriented toward traditional values, rules, or principles of proper behavior advocated by Confucian ethics. The concept *li* refers to propriety, ethics, or moral rules of proper behavior and good manners and embodies the teaching of Confucius. As a body of rules of behavior, *li* satisfies and regulates human needs and consists of family, social, and political institutions (Cao, 1999). As an essential component in Confucian ethics, *li* is considered "decency or modesty, from which ceremony originates" (Chang, 1960, p. 36). Chinese society has long valued the role of *li* in regulating social behavior, and *li* has been recognized as the proper criteria of behavior (Wen, 2005, p. 77). Confucius valued *li* and spent the best part of his life touring administrative districts, preaching to each ruler his vision of *li*. With regard to the role of *li* in regulating human behavior, Confucius (cited in Cao, 1999) remarked:

> Guide them by edicts, keep them in line with punishments and the common people will stay out of trouble but have no sense of shame. Guide them by virtue, keep them in line with rites (*li*), and they will, besides having a sense of shame, reform themselves. (p. 163)

In this sense, *li* is a "regulator of human desires that has been devised for the protection of the people"; *li* is "a form of social control over unrestrained expression of human desires"; and *li* "forbids trespasses before they are committed" (Cao, 1999, p. 164). For Confucians, society is a massive and complex system of roles in which harmony is ensured by each party honoring the requirements of the role relationships as prescribed by *li* (Bond & Hwang, 1986, p. 215). In the Confucian view, *li* shapes the governing institutions and the accepted modes of behavior in a civilized state. The broad moral principles represented in *li* have profound validity because they are rooted in innate human feelings—namely, what people in general instinctively feel to be right (Cao, 1999).

Conformism is one of the major Chinese personality traits (Lassiter, 1998). As Bond and Hwang (1986) put it, to speak of *li* is to speak of conformism — conforming to rules or norms that structure *wulun*, the Five-Cardinal Relations. Confucians believe that each party in the relationship is expected to perform his or her role in a proper way as prescribed by rules of correct behaviors. For Confucians, harmony cannot be achieved unless each party in the relationship conscientiously follows the requirements of his/her role. Failure to follow the dictates of proper role behavior would imperil the relationship and disrupt the harmony of society (Wright, 1962). This potential for disharmony is averted by inculcating a morality of compassion and righteousness upon those in positions of authority, whose violations of the moral prescriptions constitute justification for rebellion (Hsiao, 1954).

Traditionally, Confucian ethics of *li* once supplied an ideology that guided Chinese people in regard to how to live, how to organize society, and how to distinguish good from bad. Fairbank (1980), one of the leading authorities on Chinese studies, noted that Confucian ethics produced a socialized people who had a "profound moral sense of justice and proper conduct" (p. 12) and "seem[ed] to be law-abiding without law" (p. 14). The Confucian school depended on *li* to maintain the social order using moral education characterized by moral teachings, the use of persuasion, the appeal to reason and good sense, and the exemplification of good conduct and behavior (Cao, 1999, p. 164). For instance, Confucian ethics (and Taoism) supports the teaching of humility. In China, the humility of individual members is a priority for maintaining harmonious interpersonal relationships in a collectivity (Bond et al., 1982; Bond, 1986).

The literature provides evidence in this regard. Lassiter (1998) noted that Chinese families and schools stress the importance of conforming to traditional Chinese socio-moral rules (based on Confucianism), which children are expected to internalize so as to maintain proper manners (p. 73). Kleiman and Lin (1981) observed that the Chinese use moral rules as guides for behavior to a greater extent than many other cultures. Yang (1981) found that, unlike their Western counterparts, even the most rapidly modernizing segments of the Chinese population tend to act primarily in accordance with traditional Chinese socio-moral norms, along with the anticipated expectations of others, rather than with internal wishes or personal attitudes.

Yet China's modern history has experienced a crisis of faith in Confucian ethics, especially in the central values of *li* and *wulun*. In the early 20th century, much of China's educated elite—the very group that had once propagated Confucian doctrine and attempted to live by it—came to believe that it had to be abandoned if China was to survive in the modern world. This movement came to its climax in the Chinese Cultural Revolution (1966-1976), when Confucian ethics, among many other traditional value systems, became the major target of criticism full of sweeping misrepresentations and dismissive comments. However, a certain residual agreement remained regarding the qualities that make a good human being and should be nurtured in the child. Thus, *li* continues to be a strong influence in modern China, although its content has changed over time.

Chinese schools still attach as great importance as ever to fostering students' awareness of personal humility (or modesty) (Davin, 1991; Price, 1992; Zhu, 1982). For instance, modesty is among the "Five Virtues" emphasized in Chinese school curriculum and is a central criterion used to assess children's school comportment (Price, 1992). Honesty is also among the "Five Virtues," but it is mainly applicable to misdeeds. In fact, students are taught that "one should not lie about misdeeds" or "be honest with your misdeeds" (Price, 1992). In school settings, modesty is expected in both conduct and academic achievement. Children are specifically taught to avoid self-aggrandizement and not to brag about personal achievements, including high marks and good deeds, or not to seek the teacher's explicit praise. As part of the endeavor to promote modesty, self-effacement is directly encouraged (Bond et al., 1982). Children are encouraged to minimize their own good behaviors and grades and are taught to revere "unsung heroes" who commit good deeds without publicizing them.

Systematic efforts have been made to document how the socialization of children was consciously used to produce a person who is "good" according to the tenets of the dominant ideology, a person who will fulfill an appropriate, socially allocated role. Although the state also made some attempts to influence the inculcation of traditional values, rules, or principles of right conduct, it affected the socialization of children mainly through "a great range of non-family agents, extensive pre-school care, an education system that drew in the vast majority of urban children, and the Communist children's organization, the Young Pioneers" (Davin, 1991, p. 45).

Since the 1950s, the state has been making use of children's books and magazines, radio programs made specifically for the young, and later, television programs to sustain a new "children's culture" (Davin, 1991). School textbooks, radio, and TV programs are replete with stories that condone "lying" in conjunction with good deeds. Children are also encouraged to learn from the good qualities of veterans, heroes, and role models (e.g., Lei Feng, a communist hero, who carried out numerous good deeds that were discovered only after his death). The children are taught to be modest, unselfish, tidy, and polite and to serve the collective, for example, by looking after the classroom (Davin, 1991, pp. 55-56). Confucian ethics is regaining its influence in modeling Chinese culture, particularly Chinese character and social behavior, as the Chinese government attempts to promote its new agenda of constructing a society of harmony.

In summary, Chinese socio-moral culture emphasizes conformism to rules of correct behavior, which is profoundly modeled by Confucian ethics of *li* (or rules of right conduct) and characterized by sensitivity to traditional values, rules, or principles. Chinese people in general attend to the commonly recognized relevant rule or principle of correct behavior when facing questions such as "What should one do?" In pursuit of ethical solutions, when a particular answer judged to be adequate for one's self is challenged by another's "Why?", Chinese people turn to the rules or principles agreed on by the majority. In other words, they tend to justify the goodness and obligation of an act based on whether and to what extent the act is supported by relevant rules. They believe that an act is right not only by virtue of its consequences, but also because it conforms to relevant, recognized rules, and conformism to relevant rules is the core virtue of a person.

CONSIDERING RELATIONSHIP

Chinese socio-moral culture is characterized by a strong tendency to consider social consequences of threats to maintaining a positive public image and harmonious interpersonal relationships (Blum, 2007). For Confucian ethics, the ideal of social harmony is derived from the nature of humanity; the dichotomy of individual and society is barely recognized (Fingarette, 1972). Confucians believe that a human is fundamentally "a relational being, socially situated and defined within an interactive context" (Bond & Hwang, 1986, p. 215) and thus "can only be cultivated and developed in inter-human relationships in a social context" (Lin, 1974-1975, p. 193). Confucians further insist that a human exists through, and is defined by, his or her relationships to others (Bond & Hwang, 1986; Hsu, 1953). A harmonious society grows out of the kind of relations developed among particular individuals who interact with each other (Liang, 1974). For Confucians, a human is not an isolated, separate entity, but a social or interactive being (Moore, 1967, p. 5); a human cannot exist alone, but must exist in relation to others (Hu, 1944, p. 283).

The role of the Confucian tradition in shaping the Chinese culture and contouring the mentality of Chinese people has been examined by many scholars (e.g., Chen, 1989; Hsu, 1953, 1971; Markus & Kitayama, 1991; Yang, 1981). In an ethnographic study on the paradoxical relationship between teachers and students in one middle school in China, Schoenhals (1993) noted that the students were "strongly socialized to be aware of what others think of them" (p. 191) and "explicitly expected to acquire sensitivity to...other people's opinions, judgments, and evaluations" (p. 192); moreover, "failing to acquire this sensitivity has great social consequences and earns the contempt of others" (p.193). Wilson (1970, 1981), in his works on political socialization in Taiwan's primary schools, found that social opprobrium, with an element of ostracism or abandonment by the group, was a dominant moral training technique. This threat of social opprobrium was constantly manipulated by teachers and served the dual purpose of correcting the child's misdeed while simultaneously emphasizing the group's disapproval and reinforcing the rightness of the other members' behavior.

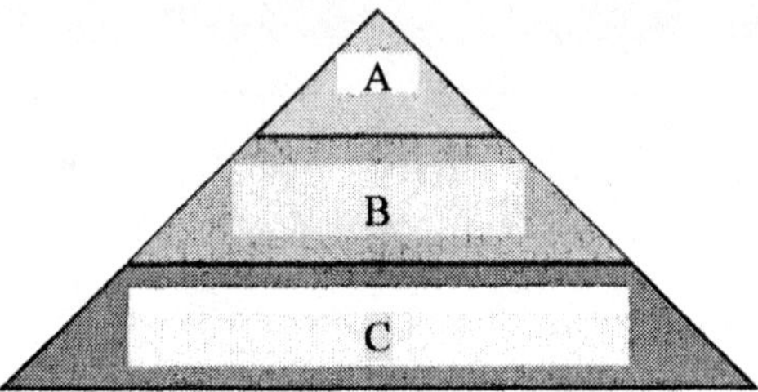

Figure 2. A "Pyramid of Chinese Morality." Adapted from Chen (1989, p. 177). A = Real Gentleman; B = False Gentleman; C = Small Man.

Another thought-provoking attempt was made by Chen (1989), a Chinese psychologist based in Taiwan. Using the perspective of the Confucian ideal of the moral "gentleman" (*junzi,* or "man of noble character"), Chen proposed a "Pyramid of Chinese Morality," defining three levels of morality (see Figure 2). At the top is the level of the "Real Gentleman" (*zhen junzi*), which is the highest stage and characteristic of "self-rule." At this level, socio-moral rules and norms are intrinsically understood and followed out of an autonomous insight into necessity rather than a blind conformity to rules. Only a very small number of people can reach this stage of self-rule or autonomy. At the bottom of the pyramid is the level of the "Small Man" (*xiaoren*), who can understand only the language of force and deterrence.

The majority of the population comprises the level of the "False Gentleman" (*wei junzi,* or hypocrites), who still possesses the potential to reach the level of the "Real Gentleman." "False" here has to do with the notion that one's adaptation to social moral rules is not entirely internalized. Rather, moral conduct of the "False Gentleman" is upheld out of fear for what those close to one would say and do if rules or norms are broken or violated. In other words, they simply "do the right thing" to become "good" in the eyes of others, and their conduct is simply a type of social performance.

From a cross-cultural perspective, Markus and Kitayama (1991) explored the differences between the self-construal of Westerners and that of Asians (e.g., Chinese, Japanese). Chinese people tend to have interdependent selves, while their Western counterparts tend to have more independent selves. Markus and Kitayama suggested that for Westerners, "self construal plays a major role in regulating various psychological processes" (p. 225). In contrast to their Western counterparts, the Chinese tend to emphasize attending to and fitting in with others as well as the importance of harmonious interdependence within a relational network. They also pointed out that, in the Chinese culture, the self is often viewed as dependent on the surrounding context; the "other" or "the self-in-relation-to-other" is at the center of individual experience, particularly individual social experience.

One general consequence of distinguishing these self-construal types is that, when psychological processes (e.g., cognition, emotion, and motivation) explicitly—or even implicitly—implicate the self as a target or as a referent, the nature of these processes will vary according to the exact form or organization of the self inherent in a given construal. For example, in regard to cognition, the Chinese perceive certain aspects of knowledge representation and the process involved in social and non-social thinking alike to be influenced by a pervasive attentiveness to the relevant others within their social context. Thus, one's actions are easily seen as situationally bound. Furthermore, for those with interdependent selves, expressions and experience of emotions and motives may be shaped by a consideration of others' verbal and non-verbal reactions.

Also from a cross-cultural perspective, Yang (1981) explored the behavioral implications of the contrast between a traditional Chinese and a modern Western position on values, attitudes, and beliefs. He found that, unlike their Western counterparts, even among the most rapidly modernizing segments of the Chinese population, the tendency exists for people to act primarily in accordance with the anticipated responses of others, along with social norms, rather than with internal wishes or personal attitudes. In integrating these differences, Yang described a continuum; at one end is what he called social orientation, the traditional Chinese pattern, while at the other end is what he labeled individual orientation, the Western pattern. Yang defined Chinese social orientation as:

> A predisposition toward such behavior patterns as social conformity, non-offensive strategy, submission to social expectations, and worry about one or more of the purposes of reward attainment, harmony maintenance, impression management, face protection, social acceptance, and avoidance of punishment, embarrassment, conflict, rejection, ridicule, and retaliation in a social situation. (p. 159)

Yang maintained that—in contrast to their Western counterparts, who place great weight on their own personal standards in deciding their behavior—Chinese people place great weight on the anticipated reactions of others to that behavior. It is others' (e.g., colleagues, friends, neighbors, peers) responses rather than their own personal standards that determine how the Chinese would act within their social network. Therefore, in the Chinese socio-cultural context, interpersonal solidarity and consciousness of social consequences of threats to interpersonal relationships are more decisive as determinants of behavior than the individuality and self-assertion dominant in Western societies.

Yang (1981) argued that the orientation toward considering social consequences "represents a tendency for a person to act in accordance with external expectations or social norms" (p. 161). A person does so, rather than act in accordance with internal wishes or personal integrity, because he would thus be able to "protect his social self and function as an integral part of the social network" (p. 161). As a result of considering social consequence, social consistency takes precedence over self-consistency. More specifically, a socially oriented person usually tends to behave in accordance with social expectations and/or role requirements at the expense of the actor's personal feelings, opinions, or will. Experience of behaving in such a way in the long run would make the actor become accustomed to a state of schism, in which the consistency and continuity between his or her social behaviors and private intentions are severed, with the latter being more or less compartmentalized from the former.

Therefore, to a person oriented toward considering social consequences of behavior, what he does or says may not mean what he feels or thinks. His external acts no longer mirror his internal states. In other words, to a social-consequence-oriented person, "family members, work groups, close friends, one's ethnic group, classmates, leaders, and so forth can become relevant references for behavioral guidelines in various situations" (Bond & Hwang, 1986, p. 222). As a result, "the enhancement of one's autonomy and self-esteem becomes secondary to, and is constrained by, the more important task of maintaining interdependence among individuals" (Fung, 1999, p. 184).

As we have seen, Chinese moral culture entails a strong orientation toward considering social consequence, which is rooted in Confucian relationalism—namely, the human as a relational being—and characterized by sensitivity to the responses or expectations of others within the relational network (Bedford & Hwang, 2003). For most—if not all—of Chinese people, an act is good and obligatory because it is most efficient and effective in producing the most wanted social consequences or meeting others' anticipation or expectations, thereby maintaining the harmony of interpersonal relationships. They believe that "the value of an act is based on its impact on significant relationships"; "wrong and right are socially defined," and action should be taken in accordance "with each circumstance, depending upon the relationships of those involved" (Bedford & Hwang, 2003, p. 133). A person who is most worthy of respect or praise is one who always gets others' positive evaluations and maintains good interpersonal relationships.

EXPRESSION OF FEELINGS

Feeling is an affective state of consciousness, such as that resulting from emotions, sentiments, or desires. Feelings are universal human psychological processes over which we have little control. Xavier (2006) posited that feelings influence our life in at least four major aspects: giving signals, providing motivation, generating pleasant or unpleasant sensations or moods, and helping modulate relationships. Specifically, feelings such as guilt, fear, or desire alert us to internal needs, external fear, or opportunities to meet a need. Feelings often move us to act, and strong feelings can motivate us to act forcefully. Feelings such as excitement, relief, and enjoyment can create good moods whereas feelings such as frustration, sadness, and anger can create bad moods; our feelings toward somebody or something can influence how we relate to that person or circumstance (pp. 52-53). Recognizing the complexity of the functioning of feelings, Xavier concluded that—in contrast to the control we have over our action and thoughts—we have less control over our feelings (p. 53).

Chinese culture has a long tradition of emphasizing the control of individual feelings. Strong faith in the goodness of human nature did not eliminate Confucian scholars' sense of the reality of human fallibility. Instead, they were aware that "human desires could overpower the goodness of the innate nature and drive one to commit evil acts—even though one knew that what one was doing violated the original goodness of one's own being" (Tillman, 1987, p. 44). In *The Analects of Confucius*, the control of feelings, needs, and desires is considered an important moral code. Confucius said, "Do not look at what is contrary to courteousness; do not listen to what is contrary to courteousness; do not speak what is contrary to courteousness; and do not do what is contrary to courteousness" (cited in Yang, 1980, p. 123; see also Wang, 2004, p. 438).

Chu Hsi (1130-1200), a leading Confucian scholar in the Song Dynasty (960-1279) and beyond, was known for his influential Confucian philosophy of reason (*lixue*), in which he conceived a person's mind as consisting of "moral mind" (*daoxin,* or *tao-hsin*) and "human mind" (*renxin,* or *jen-hsin*). According to Tu (1974), moral mind is "the ethical perfection a person's mind could achieve through a process of moral cultivation and learning" (p. 44) while human mind is conditioned by human desires or the "self-centeredness of material being" (p. 44). Tillman (1987) said that moral mind "manifests itself in total accord with moral principles" (p. 43). Meanwhile, human mind "operates existentially within the world conditioned by egocentricity: the individual's sense of self-centeredness, material needs, and human desires" (p. 43).

For Chu Hsi, the human mind is "neutral in an ethical sense. [...] Its instincts and natural desires could be educated and cultivated to conform to the ethical norms [of moral mind...and] its feelings could surge unrestrained and pursue selfish passion" (Tillman, 1987, p. 43). If a person's mind remains uncultivated and uninstructed, it would become "willfully corrupt and even bestially depraved" because the human mind is conditioned by one's "consciousness of the individual self and desires"; it would be easily driven to digress from "the moral path of moral mind" (p. 44). Therefore, control of individual self and desire is the major task of moral cultivation and instruction. Only through this regulation and self-control is the mind transformed from being desire-conditioned into a principle-governed moral mind.

Lu Chiu-Yuan (1139-1193), another influential Confucian scholar in the Song Dynasty and beyond, was renowned for his Confucian philosophy of mind (*xinxue*). Like his contemporary Confucian scholar Chu Hsi, Lu Chiu-Yuan also expressed similar awareness of the reality of human fallibility and advocated "Go to the original mind." Lu Chiu-Yuan had strong faith in the goodness of human nature. For Lu Chiu-Yuan, human nature in itself is goodness, and one's nature is complete or perfect from one's birth. Therefore, one has the innate ability to discern what is right for oneself "if one submits oneself to the authority of the mind" (Chang, 1960, p. 42). However, although in nature man is perfect or complete, he is often perplexed because he is so easily conditioned and prejudiced by his sensation, desire, passion, likes, and dislikes. Recognizing human failing, Lu Chiu-Yuan stressed the significance of "eliminating desire" in helping maintain the completeness or perfection of human nature. Consequently, "eliminating desire" is often considered one of the three principles[2] underlying Lu Chiu-Yuan's philosophy of mind. "Having few desires" becomes a vital method of self-cultivation in the traditional Chinese culture (Wang, 2004).

The emphasis on the control of feelings in the sense of desires directly impacts the way in which Chinese people express individual feelings. As documented in empirical literature, Chinese people—compared to their western counterparts—are more reserved in revealing personal feelings in the presence of others. In the Chinese socio-moral context, a person who can control his or her feelings is perceived as being socially and morally mature. This is especially true for older children (Kao & Landreth, 2000, p. 48). As noted earlier, Yang (1981) found that even the most rapidly modernizing segments of the Chinese population rarely act in accordance with internal wishes or personal attitudes. Bond (1993) found that, compared with that in western culture, the expression of emotions in Chinese culture is characterized by low frequency, low intensity, and short duration. Bond also observed that the Chinese "expression of emotion is carefully regulated out of concern for its capacity to disrupt group harmony and status hierarchies" (p. 245).

This cultural emphasis on emotional control was strengthened and institutionalized by the Chinese Communist Party. When it came into power in

---

[2] The other two principles are "To establish what is fundamental or great" and "Not to consider knowledge-seeking as of prime importance." For details, please refer to Chang (1960, pp. 42-43).

1949, the Chinese Communist Party started taking heavy-handed efforts to control cultural production and the service sector, strictly defining taste as well as restricting and denigrating leisure-time activities. This institutionalized effort reached its extreme during the Cultural Revolution (1966-1976), when only a limited number of entertainment products passed official muster (Gold, 1993). Music, film, operas, radio programs, and—above all—literature at all times and in all countries were never allowed to circulate without approvals or permits issued by governing ministries of the central government.

Nonetheless, when I talk about the fact that the Chinese Communist Party and the Cultural Revolution added to the traditional emphasis on the control of personal feelings, I do not forget that, by the same coin, another side always exists and may be not as shiny. Wang Shuo, a popular writer of more than 20 books, once wrote, "No matter how bad the Cultural Revolution was made out to be, it disrupted the orderliness of everyday life and offered opportunities for individual development and freed the children from the bonds of the old and decaying education [system]" (Wang, 1992, p. 34). Thus, the Cultural Revolution provided a unique environment for youngsters, especially those of "the political elite to develop a youth counterculture that contradicted Mao's aim to empower them for making revolution" (Yao, 2004, p. 431). Consequently, those former aristocratic youths who failed to join the new elite became marginalized and impoverished in the post-Mao era. They tried to adapt to and show their existence in the new environment of growing commercialism and materialism by developing an irreverent, playful attitude toward authority as well as an intuitive attitude toward knowing.

These marginalized aristocratic youths' countercultural characteristics—namely, rebellion, irreverence, daring, cleverness, street-smarts, authenticity, and self-importance—further expressed and legitimized the desires and frustrations of the ordinary urban youths, who also felt marginalized and alienated, and who wanted to subvert the "sham, inflated, and empty" (*jia da kong*) dominant culture (Yao, 2004). Youngsters, no matter how mildly deviant or radically disaffected, feel that it is "cool" to identify with countercultural characteristics, adopting an irreverent, playful attitude toward authority and an intuitive attitude toward knowing. For many of them, the only thing that is real is their own feelings—namely, their sentiments, needs, and desires.

This youth counterculture movement originating during the Cultural Revolution gained momentum as China practiced its "Reform and Opening-up" strategy in the late 1970s. Since then, cultural imports—first from peripheral areas such as Hong Kong and Taiwan and subsequently from western countries, especially the United States—have entered into the life of Chinese people and added fresh elements to the leisure-time activities of Chinese people in general and youngsters in particular. These cultural imports are intensely personal and convey to the young generations a striking sense of fun and relaxation.

As Gold (1993) pointed out, the cultural imports express individual emotions and are related to actual life as opposed to abstract concepts; they concentrate on small incidents and feelings with which people can identify. The cultural imports are able to capture and influence the youngsters who have been trying to puzzle out the "sham, inflated, and empty" dominant ideology and culture. Imported music, film, television shows, literature, advertisements, décor, attire, and leisure have all demonstrated their appeal to the mainland Chinese by advocating the free expression of individual emotions, needs, and desires. They have provided the majority of ordinary Chinese people, especially young people, with a selection of alternative life styles or models. As a result, a new discourse has broken the hegemonic lock of traditional values and modern ideology and begun to empower young generations to express their own feelings and pursue their needs and desires (Goldfarb, 1989). Just as the pop song lyrics "Go with Your Feelings" (cited in Gold, 1993) stated:

Go with your feelings
Tightly grasp your dream hand
Footsteps grow lighter and lighter
Livelier and livelier
With all your emotions, spread around your smile

Love can grasp me at any place. (p. 914)

As we can see, Chinese socio-moral culture has a long tradition of emphasizing the control of individual feelings, and Chinese people in general are reserved in expressing individual feelings and desires. It can be anticipated that many Chinese people would, consciously or unconsciously, not turn to personal feelings or desires while justifying ethical conduct in front of other people in order to show their maturity of self-cultivation.

However, recent socio-cultural developments in China have opened the gateway for Chinese youngsters to express their own feelings in given situations and to pursue their needs, desires, and passions. Oriented to the intuitive moral sense, they no longer try to control their feelings, but rather submit themselves to the authority of their own feelings and intuited knowledge. For Chinese youngsters, orientation to personal feelings, needs, or desires is no longer shameful; instead, personal feelings, needs, and desires are those by and for which they exist. "Go with your feelings" has become an approach to knowledge and a guide for action (Yao, 2004).

In moral dilemmas, more and more Chinese youngsters have begun to attend to their feelings, sensitivity, and intuition. In posing the moral question "What should I do?", they would ask "What's happening?" or "What is the situation like?" Their answers are expected to be in such forms of discourse as: "I just want (or I just do not want) to do so and so"; "I just like (or I just do not like) to do such and such"; "I feel good/bad to do so and so"; and "I feel it is most fitting to the situation to do such and such." For youngsters, an act is more likely perceived as good because it constitutes not only the most appropriate or honest expression of their self and feelings, but also the most fitting response to the situation in which their self exists. Sensitivity to personal feelings in the sense of emotion, sentiments, and desires makes a person look "real" and, consequently, most worthy of respect and honor.

CHAPTER 2
Methodology

People know what they do; they frequently know why they do what they do; but what they don't know is what what they do does.

—Michel Foucault (1988)

The present study was carried out in two major phases: the pilot study and the main study. In this chapter, I will first review the pilot study, illuminating its purposes, procedures, and results, then detail the main study, explaining the rationale for the research design and introducing the means and procedures of data collection, coding, and analysis. Finally, I will discuss validity issues.

THE PILOT STUDY

The main purpose of the pilot study was to test the questionnaire and the interview protocols, which are the major research instruments of the main study. As the main study will involve one group interview and two individual interviews, the pilot study also sought to determine whether the group interview should be conducted before, between, or after the two individual interviews.

Twenty-five sixth graders (including 11 boys and 14 girls) volunteered to participate in the pilot study. They were all selected from a primary school in Beijing. Participants were introduced to the nature, purpose, and procedures of the pilot study. Informed consent was obtained from the students and their parents. The data collecting took almost one month, starting in early October and ending by early November 2006. Participants first completed a questionnaire and then participated in interviews. To minimize "informational social influence" (Aronson, Wilson, & Akert, 2005), participants were also instructed not to share with other participants and non-participants what they conveyed or talked about in the questionnaire and interviews.

The participants (n = 25) completed a Chinese questionnaire translated from its English version (which will be introduced later in the main study). The analysis of their responses revealed that 16 students (8 boys and 8 girls) expressed positive interest in participating in continuing tasks (group and individual interviews); the remaining 9 students (3 boys and 6 girls) were either only interested in the group interview or not interested in any tasks at all. The analysis also found that respondents who showed interest in both group and individual interviews were able to understand the meanings of lying and truth-telling and were able to satisfy at least one of the three criteria for participation: (a) being able to tell an autobiographic story of lying about good deeds; (b) being able to tell a story about others' lying about good deeds; and/or (c) being able to recollect some socialization experiences concerning lying about good deeds in various contexts.

Therefore, I decided to use the 16 students who indicated that they were interested in both the group and individual interviews as focal participants for the pilot study. These 16 students were divided into 3 groups, each of which would try one of the three variations in the sequence of interviews: GP[3]—IN1—IN2, IN1—IN2—GP, and IN1—GP—IN2.

Another major decision based on the analysis of the children's responses to the questionnaire was that the questionnaire as a whole is good for use as the first part of the data collection in the main study, although it needed tweaking.

[3] GP is short for Group Interview, IN1 for Individual Interview No. 1, and IN2 for Individual Interview No. 2.

The necessary modifications did not stem from the quality of the questionnaire *per se*, but from the Chinese translation. Specifically, questions 8 through 11 in the Chinese version of the questionnaire needed rewording so that they could be clearly understood by Chinese participants. It should be noted that I do not believe that tweaks are needed for the English version.

The 16 boys and girls who showed strong interest in participating in the remaining research tasks were invited to participate in interviews; however, 4 students did not show up for physical reasons. Therefore, the 12 students (5 boys and 7 girls) were randomly assigned to 3 sessions, each consisting of 4 students. The interview sequences or modes for Sessions 1, 2, and 3 were GP—IN1—IN2, IN1—IN2—GP, and IN1—GP—IN2, respectively.

Session 1 (GP—IN1—IN2) included 1 boy and 3 girls. The group interview went very well. Each of the 4 participants had a chance to speak, although the girls seemed to be slightly more talkative than the boy. However, during individual interviews, participants seemed to be stuck around the major points discussed during the group interview. For example, in the group interview, participants discussed the question "What do you think he or she was feeling about when he or she conducted that good deed?" They suggested that the doer of the good deed was feeling happy, comfortable, glad, and/or proud. When they were individually interviewed, they unexceptionally used only these previously mentioned words to express their own feelings about doing good deeds.

In addition, during the group interview, when participants were asked whether they had heard or read about any story in which someone conducted good deeds without taking credit, they mentioned Lei Feng, a household Chinese hero of moral nobility. During the subsequent individual interview, when they were asked about their reading or schooling experiences whereby they learned about "not taking credit for doing good deeds," the only character mentioned was Lei Feng. Although it is unclear whether their responses in individual interviews were associated with the information they obtained from the group interview, it is uncertain to what extent their responses in individual interviews reflected their own thoughts. With this thought in mind, I decided to try out Session 2, conducting individual interviews before the group interview.

Session 2 (IN1—IN2—GP) included 2 boys and 2 girls. Each student was individually interviewed twice before all of them gathered for the group interview. The two individual interviews went well; each participant answered my interview questions in detail regarding personal experiences and knowledge as well as some common experiences in schooling. When they were asked about reading or schooling experiences in which they learned about "not taking credit for doing good deeds," two students mentioned Lei Feng, one student mentioned both Lei Feng and Ouyang Hai (another household name in China), and another one mentioned a TV program about a teenager who saved a one-year-old baby who dropped into a 13-meter deep well but did not take credit for this heroic behavior. This diversity of students' responses was striking.

Later, in the group interview, all the participants were very active and offered more information. For example, in Session 1's group interview, all the discussions were focused on the questions I had prepared. However, in Session 2's group interview, not only were all the prepared questions fully discussed, but several fresh stories also emerged. Participants even mentioned a good deed conducted by one group member and discussed its moral significance for other students in their class. At this moment, I realized that this procedure of interviews was more likely to ensure the reliability of the research, although I decided to try out Session 3 before making a final decision.

Session 3 (IN1—GP—IN2) also included 2 boys and 2 girls. First, each of them participated in the first individual interview; then, all of the session members attended the group interview. Finally, each of them participated in the second individual interview. The two individual interviews went very well. Although the group interview did not affect the quality of the second individual interview, it as a whole was far from satisfactory. During the first 10 minutes or so, students were excitedly exchanging their feelings about the first individual interview and thus barely responded to my interview questions. I tried very hard to finally pull them back to "stay the course" and get some of the interview questions discussed. Moreover, much more time was required to complete this group interview than in Sessions 1 and 2.

Having completed all three sessions, I listened to the audio data to verify my initial impressions obtained from the pilot study, which strengthened my positive impression of the second sequence or mode of interviewing—namely, group interview following the two individual interviews. Using this mode of interviewing, each participant seemed more likely to respond to the individual interviewing questions based on their personal experiences, knowledge, and understanding. They were also more likely to deepen their group discussion by incorporating more details and richer information. I was also able to present the whole group with some questions not as fully discussed in the individual interviews so that they could use "distributive intelligence" (Perkins, 1992, p. 133) and help co-construct their discussions.

Ultimately, I concluded that Session 2's interview mode, namely, IN1—IN2—GP, would be used for the data collection of the main study. In addition, in accordance with the piloting results, the Chinese versions of the questionnaire and interview protocols were fine-tuned to ensure the reliability of these instruments when used in the main study.

THE MAIN STUDY

RESEARCH SITE

This study was conducted in Beijing, the capital city of China. The selection of Beijing as a research site, although somewhat arbitrary, was due primarily to practical considerations. Before coming to the United States, I had lived and taught in Beijing for years and had thus established good personal and professional relationships with local educational authorities, school leaders, and classroom teachers. These relationships helped me gain access to educational institutions at all levels without much difficulty. In the process of gathering schools as research sites, I received assistance from former colleagues, friends, and college alumni who were now either university faculty, K-12 teachers at local public schools, or leaders at the Beijing Municipal Education Committee, the city's top educational authority.

The selection of Beijing as a research site also stemmed from a participant-diversity consideration. Using Beijing made it more likely that students of diverse backgrounds would be included in the sample. Beijing distinguishes itself by functioning as both the center of Chinese politics, economy, and culture and a nexus of international information flow. Therefore, youngsters living in a metropolitan city like Beijing are more likely to be exposed to, and construct meanings of, modes of diverse thoughts, attitudes, and values. Indeed, Beijing hosts a diverse student population. Of the 17 million people in Beijing, up to 30% (5.1 million persons) are part of the large labor force migrating from other provinces to Beijing for job opportunities or business (The Associated Press, 2007). These "migrant workers"[4] brought to Beijing not only their dreams of careers and fortunes, but also their family and school-aged children. These children of "migrant workers" diversified the geographical composition of the city's student population as well as enriched the modes of thoughts, attitudes, and values among its residents.

---

[4] According to Congressional-Executive Commission on China (n.d.), the term "migrant worker" has to do with China's *hukou* (household registration) system, which—since its institution in the 1950s—has imposed strict limits on ordinary Chinese citizens changing their permanent place of residence. Beginning with the reform period in the late 1970s and accelerating during the late 1990s, national and local authorities relaxed restrictions on obtaining urban residence permits. Since the late 1990s, Chinese authorities have deepened and expanded prior *hukou* reforms, which included relaxing limitations on migration to small towns and cities, streamlining *hukou* registration in some provinces and large cities, and instituting many individual reforms aimed at addressing the abuse of migrants. Since late 2004, central authorities have also made efforts to eliminate discriminatory local regulations that limit urban employment prospects for migrants. For details of the Chinese *hukou* system and related reforms, see Wang (2005).

This study was conducted in two public schools: Pacific Primary School[5] and Font High School. While still in the United States, I started contacting leaders and teachers of public schools located in Beijing, introducing to them the research project and explaining that it seeks to understand Chinese students' encountering and meaning-making of attitudes and practices around "doing good deeds without leaving one's name." Of all the schools I contacted, Pacific Elementary School and Font High School expressed the most supportive interest in the research project.

Shortly after returning to Beijing in late September 2006, I paid my first visit to Pacific Primary School and obtained official permission from its principal and other relevant faculty and administrators to conduct the present study there. Ms. Yang, a moral educator and director of the Young Pioneers League [6] of the school, assumed the role of official coordinator for the study. She helped me contact students and their parents to gather their informed consent, schedule class visits, distribute and collect questionnaires, and reserve rooms for interviews, among other activities.

Pacific Primary School, located in downtown Beijing, is an "average school"[7] with approximately 600 boys and girls enrolled in 24 classes, from grades 1 to 6. Class size ranges from some 20 to 30 students. According to Ms. Yang, just a few years ago students studying at Pacific Elementary School came mostly from families of permanent Beijing residents. However, with the recent introduction of a new admission policy, local public schools—mainly average schools—began accepting "migrant students." Of the students currently enrolled in Pacific Elementary School, more than 60% were from families of migrant

---

[5] All the names of both schools and human subjects are pseudonyms, unless otherwise clarified.

[6] Young Pioneers League, a national youth organization, consists of children between the ages of 6 and 14 and advances various tasks, such as guiding youths to participate in various activities of social, moral, and political significance or implication.

[7] China's public schools are often categorized as *putong xuexiao* (average schools) and *zhongdian xuexiao* (key schools). Average schools usually receive relatively limited resources from government, and their students mostly come from under-represented or less advantaged families. In contrast, key schools usually receive admirable resources from public sectors and enroll students mostly from families of privileged cliques and social classes.

workers, with the rest coming from underprivileged families of permanent Beijing residents.

I next visited Font High School and obtained permission to conduct the study there. Ms. Wang, a moral educator and director of the school's Division of Political Education, was officially assigned as coordinator for the present study. Font High School, located in southwest Beijing City proper, is also an average school, enrolling approximately 2,200 students in grades 7 to 12. Class size ranges from 40 to 60 students. According to Ms. Wang, approximately 10% of the students in Font High School are children of migrant workers, while the majority of the students are from families of Beijing permanent residents. Of the students with Beijing *hukou*, up to 80% are second- or third-generation migrants from all over the country who have come to Beijing to study or train, get married or join family, and/or serve in the military forces or public sectors. In addition, approximately 15% are children of the "Educated Youth"[8] who went to work in the countryside and mountain areas during the Cultural Revolution, subsequently returning to Beijing. Of the 48 ninth graders the present study sampled, 5 were living with non-parent relatives (e.g., grandparents, uncles, and aunts) while their parents were living in remote provinces, such as Yunnan and Xinjiang. Font High School was also an "average school," but was recognized as being above average by the students sampled in this study.

---

[8] The "Educated Youth," also known in Chinese as *zhishi qingnian* or simply *zhiqing*, is a household term in China that refers to a particular group of people in its modern history. The original meaning of *zhiqing* was to indicate a knowledgeable youth or a young person who had received a high level of education. However, the most common usage today is in regard to young people who, from the 1950s until the end of the Cultural Revolution, willingly or under coercion left urban areas and were rusticated to rural areas to assume peasant lives. The vast majority of those who went had received elementary to high school education. A small minority had matriculated to the post-secondary or higher level. In 1977, university entrance exams were reinstated, inspiring the majority of the "Educated Youth" to attempt to return to the cities. On October 1, 1980, China decided to end the movement and allow the youth to return to their families in the cities. In addition, following age restrictions, one child per family of the "Educated Youth" was permitted to accompany their parent(s) to their native cities. Throughout the period, from the 1950s to the end of the 1970s, an estimated 12 to 18 million youth became rusticated *zhiqing*. By the time of the present research study, most children of China's "Educated Youth" were expected to be in their 20s or 30s, and only a small proportion of them were teenagers whose parent(s) went to work in the countryside and mountain areas in the late 1970s. For a detailed discussion on this population, please refer to Singer (1971).

PARTICIPANTS

Age range. 7-, 9-, 12-, and 15-year-old children participated in the present study. This relatively wide age range was based upon an understanding of its necessity and feasibility. First of all, it is believed that a relatively wide age range would make it possible for us to see various ways in which children construct meanings with increased exposure to various attitudes and practices related to reporting good deeds. In addition, it has been documented that 7-year-olds were ready to talk about personal experiences with rich elaboration (Fivush & Hudson, 1990; Han, Leichtman, & Wang, 1998; Nelson, 1996) and with complete and complex scenes (Sutton-Smith, 1981; Tucker, 1995) while 15-year-old children's ethical discourse approximated adults' (Fang et al., 2003; Fu et al., 2001). Moreover, 9- and 12-year-olds were sampled simply because doing so, as I anticipated, might help differentiate the patterns of ethical discourse. Therefore, all 7-, 9-, 12-, and 15-year-olds (who in theory were expected to be second, fourth, sixth, and ninth [9] graders, respectively) were invited to participate in this exploration.

Primary participants. An invitation sent to all 290 second, fourth, sixth, and ninth graders in the two selected schools received positive reply from 186 students, who were thus selected to be the primary participants. As presented in Table 1, the primary participants included 45 second graders (28 boys and 17 girls), 40 fourth graders (28 boys and 12 girls), 53 sixth graders (29 boys and 24 girls), and 48 ninth graders (26 boys and 22 girls).

The mean ages (standard deviation indicated in parenthesis) of second-, fourth-, sixth-, and ninth-grade primary participants are 7.32 (0.36), 9.47 (0.70), 11.85 (0.57), and 14.73 (0.62). The second-, fourth-, and sixth-grade participants are from Pacific Elementary School while the ninth-grade participants are from

[9] In China, people seldom use the term ninth grade(r); instead, they use "third grade(r) of junior high school" (*chuzhong san nianji*). In order to be consistent with current English literature, in this book, ninth grade(r) is used to represent third grade(r) of junior high school in China.

Font High School. Of the 186 participants, 111 (60%) are males, and 75 (40%) are females; the difference is statistically significant (t = 5.4; p < = .05)[10]. All 186 participants responded to the questionnaire (which will be detailed later). Hereafter, I will refer to these 186 questionnaire respondents as the primary participants or primary sample.

Table 1

Distribution of Primary Participants by Gender and Age (n = 186)

Grade	n	Gender		Age				
		Boy (%)	Girl (%)	Mean	SD	Range	Min	Max
2nd	45	28 (62%)	17(38%)	7.32	0.36	1.41	6.92	8.33
4th	40	28 (70%)	12(30%)	9.47	0.70	3.42	8.08	11.50
6th	53	29 (55%)	24(45%)	11.85	0.57	3.09	10.83	13.92
9th	48	26 (54%)	22(46%)	14.73	0.62	3.16	13.17	16.33
Total	186	111(60%)	75(40%)	—	—	—	—	—

Focal participants. From the primary sample, I subsequently selected a focal group of 41 students (see Table 2), who participated in in-depth individual and group interviews. The rationale for selecting a focal group is grounded in what developmental researchers term the optimum of developmental outcome (Li, 2002). Just as Chase (2006) has so elegantly put it, "The human way of life is shaped by culture (p. 1). Child development is viewed as a product of what Lightfoot and Valsiner (1992) and Valsiner (1988) labeled "societal culture" or "collective culture." Accordingly, cultures have a preferred, desirable "endpoint" (Bruner, 1986; Rogers, 1969) or "optimal ways of being" (Csikszentmihalyi & Rathunde, 1998, p. 639) toward which younger members of a culture are enculturated. To be sure, enculturation does not produce one-to-one mirror correspondence between a given cultural model and members of the culture, but

[10] The present study used .05 as the level of significance, unless otherwise clarified.

eventuates in individuals' varied appropriations of the cultural model (Spiro, 1987; Strauss, 1992). Nevertheless, it is important to describe the optimal development of ethical discourse on lying about good deeds as it exists in Chinese people's minds and guides their behavior (D'Andrade, 1992; Harkness & Super, 1996).

Table 2

Distribution of Focal Participants by Gender and Age (n = 41)

Grade	n	Gender		Age				
		Boy (%)	Girl (%)	Mean	SD	Range	Min	Max
2nd	11	5 (45%)	6 (55%)	7.51	0.45	1.41	6.92	8.33
4th	08	3 (37%)	5 (63%)	9.23	0.46	1.49	8.18	9.67
6th	12	6 (50%)	6 (50%)	12.33	0.74	2.42	11.50	13.92
9th	10	5 (50%)	5 (50%)	14.67	0.69	2.50	13.83	16.33
Total	41	19(46%)	22(54%)	—	—	—	—	—

Focal participants were selected based on four basic criteria: (a) interest in participating in interviews; (b) reasonable judgment about whether an utterance is true or false and whether a deed is good or bad; (c) personal experience in lying about good deeds; and (d) knowledge of others' attitudes and practices related to reporting good deeds. The identification of an optimal focal participant was based on his/her responses to questionnaire items.

First, a basic group was defined, consisting of those who matched Criterion 1. From this group, those who scored negatively on Criteria 2, 3, and/or 4 were excluded. Based on this screening, 41 focal participants were selected, including 11 (out of 45) second graders, 8 (out of 40) fourth graders, 12 (out of 53) sixth graders, and 10 (out of 48) ninth graders, as presented in Table 2. This focal sample consisted of 19 boys (46%) and 22 girls (54%). The gender difference is not statistically significant (t = 1.08; p = .32). The mean ages (standard deviation indicated in parenthesis) of second-, fourth-, sixth-, and ninth-grade focal participants are 7.51 (0.45), 9.23 (0.46), 12.33 (0.74), and 14.67 (0.69), respectively. In contrast to the primary sample or primary participants, these 41 students are hereafter referred to as the focal sample or focal participants. Each focal participant was first individually interviewed twice and then participated in a group interview along with other focal participants from his or her age group.

Table 3

Sibling and Family Socio-Economic Status of Focal Participants (n = 41)

Grade	n	Sibling Status		Family Socio-Economic Status			
		OC (%)	NOC (%)	JP (%)	LI (%)	MI (%)	HI (%)
2nd	11	7 (64%)	4 (36%)	1 (9%)	8 (73%)	1 (9%)	1 (9%)
4th	08	6 (75%)	2 (25%)	0	7 (88%)	0	1(12%)
6th	12	7 (58%)	5 (42%)	1 (8%)	8 (67%)	3 (25%)	0
9th	10	8 (80%)	2 (20%)	0	3 (30%)	4 (40%)	3(30%)
Total	41	28(68%)	13 (32%)	2 (5%)	26(63%)	8 (20%)	5(12%)

Note: OC = only child; NOC = non-only child; JP = jobless parents; LI = low income; MI = middle income; HI = high income.

Table 3 depicts information about sibling and family socio-economic status of the focal participants. According to the data, 28 (68%) of the focal participants (n = 41) are the only child[11] in their family while 13 (32%) have one or more siblings. In terms of socio-economic status, 2 (5%) reported that their parents (both father and mother) were jobless. Meanwhile, 26 (63%) came from low-income families, with their parents mainly working as taxi drivers, cleaners,

[11] In 1979, the One-Child Policy was first introduced to China. This policy was enforced nationwide beginning in 1981. The One-Child Policy called for enforcing laws allowing each couple within China to have just one child. The enforcement of this policy eventuates in the emergence of the "Only Child" phenomenon in Chinese society. I included data on sibling status simply to suggest the variety of the focal sample; I did not look at whether and/or how sibling status was associated with children's ethical discourse.

construction workers, or manufacturing workers; 8 (20%) came from middle-income families, with their parents working mostly as police, teachers, civic servants, or accountants; and 5 (12%) came from high-income families, with parents working as lawyers, doctors, business managers, or CEOs.

RESEARCH INSTRUMENTS

To generate data and answer the overarching research questions, the questionnaire and interviews were employed as major research instruments. I also collected various school documents about evaluating and rewarding students' social and moral behaviors. In addition, I kept field notes about my observations of the school ecology, free talks with school leaders and teachers, and thoughts and feelings emerging during each phase of the research study. The following discussions detail these instruments.

Questionnaire. The questionnaire was administered mainly to gather information for (a) selecting focal participants, (b) revising interview protocols, and (c) informing the overarching research questions. Accordingly, the questionnaire was constructed by incorporating my questions with questions from existing studies and was subsequently revised based on the pilot study results. This questionnaire consists of five sections, all of which work toward obtaining preparatory information for the interviews while each assumes a distinct objective.

1. Section I aims to gather participants' background information. It includes five questions concerning participants' age, gender, residence status (*hukou*), parents' occupation, and family financial status.
2. Section II entails two questions that aim to gather information pertaining to participants' conceptual understanding of the truthfulness (or falsehood) of an utterance and whether a behavior is ethically good or bad.

3. Section III aims to gather information to shed light on students' experiential knowledge of lying about good deeds. This section includes three questions asking about participants', peers', and role models' attitudes and practices related to reporting good deeds. Answers to these questions provided major information for determining focal participants and revising interview questions.
4. Section IV aims to gather information about students' moral statements about the rightness or wrongness of lying about good deeds in various settings. This section includes two hypothetical stories borrowed from existing studies (e.g., Lee et al., 1997, 2001). Story 1 involves a child character who lied to her teacher about a good deed she had done on campus. Story 2 involves a child character who lied to his teacher about a good deed he had done off campus.
5. Section V consists of only one question, asking primary participants to state their interest in taking part in the remaining research tasks—namely, group and individual interviews.

The questionnaire was first constructed in English (Appendix A) and then translated into Chinese. Back-translation was used to reduce mistranslation. A research assistant translated the Chinese version back into English and then compared it with the original English version. The comparison suggested that both versions convey the same information. Based on the pilot results (as introduced earlier in this chapter), I revised the questionnaire by rewording some of the questions to make them culturally and developmentally comprehensible to the primary participants. In the main study, all primary participants responded to the revised Chinese version of the questionnaire.

Interview. The interview serves as the major data source of this research. It consists of two sections: individual interviews and group interviews by grade[12]. Although both sections pursue a common purpose of eliciting participants' ethical

[12] As noted earlier, the focal sample includes 41 children selected from four grades (second, fourth, sixth, and ninth). Focal participants from the same grade constitute one group. I thus organized four groups, each of which was collectively interviewed once.

discourse, each has distinct objectives. Individual interview sought to provide each focal participant an environment in which he or she felt comfortable to generate story narratives by recalling his or her experiences with various attitudes and practices around reporting good deeds as well as articulating the ethical meanings of these stories. The individual interview entailed two stages: Individual Interview No. 1 (IN1) and Individual Interview No. 2 (IN2).

Dividing the individual interview into two stages was based on two considerations. First, children—especially younger ones—might otherwise feel overwhelmed as the whole interview process was expected to require up to an hour. Second, each stage had its own distinct objectives. Specifically, IN1 (Appendix B) was focused on, but not limited to, eliciting children's recollections of lived *experiences* related to encounters with and meaning-making of attitudes and practices of lying about good deeds. In this stage, participants were encouraged to generate story narratives based on personal, peers', and role models' practices of lying about good deeds. In contrast, IN2 (Appendix C) was focused on, but not limited to, eliciting children's *reflections* about their lived experiences related to encounters with and meaning-making of attitudes and practices of lying about good deeds. During this stage, participants made cognitive, affective, and conative reflections about personal, peers', and role models' attitudes and practices of lying about good deeds as well as made moral and ethical arguments about specific practices of lying about good deeds.

In either stage of the individual interviews, four major questions were asked, each followed with a number of probe questions helping students recall specifics of generated story narratives. The first question focused on participants' personal experiences, asking students to recall their own behavior of lying about good deeds. The second question focused on participants' interactive experiences, asking them to recall an experience in which they were exposed to others'—especially peers' or friends'—expressed attitudes and/or practical behaviors related to reporting good deeds. The third question focused on participants' social learning experiences, asking them to recall an experience whereby they had access to a role model's or a public figure's expressed attitudes and/or practical behaviors of lying about good deeds. The fourth question sought to elicit participants' moral and ethical arguments about practical behaviors of lying about good deeds.

As with the questionnaire, the interview protocols were first developed in English and then translated into Chinese. Next, the guest translator put the Chinese version back into English and compared with the original English version. We again agreed that both versions of the interview protocols asked the same questions. The Chinese version of interview questions was piloted and revised based on the piloting results; some of the questions were reworded so as to make them more comprehensible to the students. In the main study, all participants were interviewed in Mandarin Chinese.

Group interviews (Appendix D) aimed to provide focal participants from each age group an environment in which they felt comfortable to complement and extend the details of certain story narratives generated during individual interviews. It also sought to some degree to triangulate the story narratives generated in individual interviews. The rationale for conducting group interviews is based on the theory of distributive intelligence, which holds that "people think and remember socially, through interaction with other people, sharing information and perspectives and developing ideas" (Perkins, 1992, pp. 133-134).

Three major questions were asked, each followed by probing questions. Question 1 aimed to engage participants in constructive dialogues to recall details of a specific event concerning reporting good deeds. Question 2 sought to elicit participants' meaning-making of the way(s) in which practical behaviors of lying about good deeds were treated by persons or institutions of authority. Question 3 invited participants to dialectically discuss the pros and cons of reporting a good deed.

Again, the group interview protocol was first developed in English and then translated into Chinese. Back translation was again employed to ensure the reliability of the Chinese translation. Based on the piloting results, I revised the questions, which were not finalized until the completion of both the questionnaire and the individual interviews. Although major questions for all age groups remained consistent in nature, specific probe questions varied with different age groups due to the fact that different age groups often generated different story narratives.

Additional instruments. Relevant school documents were also collected to help me better understand the context in which participants were exposed to the rules and norms concerning lying about good deeds. These school documents included (a) copies of written texts concerning moral evaluation criteria, procedures, and reward management and (b) samples of notebooks with records of students who carried out good deeds and how they were treated by persons and/or institutions of authority. Field notes were kept to record (a) my thoughts and feelings about each phase of the study; (b) free talks about school leaders, teachers, and students; and (c) observations of the school ecology in which students live, learn, and interact. These field notes informed my understanding and interpretation of the collected survey and interview data.

PROCEDURES

To gather a primary sample, 290 invitations along with a parent informed consent form were sent to the parents or guardians of targeted students; 231 copies of the parent informed consent form were returned with permission to administer the questionnaire to their children. Next, 231 copies of the invitation along with a student informed consent form were distributed to the students whose parents or guardians had granted permission. Eventually, 186 students returned their informed consent form with agreement to be the primary participants and complete the questionnaire.

The questionnaire was first administered in Pacific Primary School. To eliminate the possibility of cross-influence, all interested second, fourth, and sixth graders completed the questionnaire during the same class meeting time[13] in their own classrooms under the direction and supervision of their *banzhuren* (class advisor or head teacher), who had received training for this research task. The same strategy was applied to the interested ninth graders in Font High School. Students of one school did not know those of the other school and had no chance to communicate about the present study. Each student of the selected grades received a copy of the questionnaire; only those who were willing to participate in the study completed the questionnaire, with those who were unwilling to participate studying on their own. I walked around and answered questions from the students who were completing the questionnaire. The fourth, sixth, and ninth graders did not report difficulty in understanding the questionnaire, while the second graders were read each item of the questionnaire by their class advisors. The fourth, sixth, and ninth graders completed the questionnaire in 20 to 30 minutes, while the second graders did it in the scheduled 45 minutes, including the time class advisors spent reading the questionnaire items.

Based on the preliminary analysis of relevant questionnaire data, I finalized the interview questions and selected a focal sample of 41 students based on the information pertaining to the four major questions in the questionnaire. Then, another parent informed consent form was sent to the parents of the 41 focal participants, all of whom granted permission to interview their children. Afterwards, another student informed consent form was distributed to the selected students, all of whom agreed to participate in the interviews.

The interviews—both individual and group—were carried out at the students' convenience and spanned approximately three months. The individual interviews started in early November 2006 and ended in mid-January 2007. Each

---

[13] Each class in Chinese schools usually holds weekly *banhui* (literally, class meeting), organized by *banzhuren* (class advisor or head teacher) during the same class period on Monday or Friday afternoon. During *banhui*, class advisors mainly summarize students' performance during the past week, announce plans and requirements for the coming week, and/or organize the whole class to discuss or participate in important school/class activities.

individual interview lasted from 20 to 40 minutes, plus 5 to 10 minutes of "warm-up" (i.e., free chat with the interviewee). In general, interviews with the second and fourth graders lasted approximately 20 minutes, while those with the sixth and ninth graders lasted around 30 minutes, with a few exceptions (mainly the ninth graders) running up to 40 minutes or even longer. The group interviews were conducted in late January 2007, once all individual interviews had been completed. Based on preliminary analysis of the questionnaire data and thoughts emerging in the individual interviews, the group interview questions were finalized. The group interviews with each group were carried out at different time periods. Each interview lasted approximately 30 to 40 minutes, plus about 5 to 10 minutes of warm-up (i.e., free chat).

I conducted the interviews by following the interview questions while simultaneously prodding participants to think and talk more using the "Tell me more" strategy (Duckworth, 2001). When encouraged to "tell me more," students indeed tended to talk more and include more details. I also allowed them to talk freely about things related to their life, schools, thoughts, and feelings. Both the individual and group interviews went very well. Students in individual interviews showed great interest in participating in this study and were ready conversationalists. In group interviews, students were more active and talkative than expected. It seems that current Chinese students—at least those living in the cities—are becoming increasingly confident and willing to speak up in public. Even those who were initially shy opened up quickly and talked freely with group members and me. All group interviews were full of enthusiastic debates and exchanges of ideas.

All the interviews were audio-recorded. While having planned to video-record the group interviews, I was unable to get permission to do so; therefore, the group interviews were audio-recorded. Concerned about how to identify the speakers while transcribing the group interviews, I applied two strategies to cope with the issue of the absence of visual image. First, it was agreed that anyone who wanted to talk should state his or her name before speaking so that his/her identification information was audio-recorded. In addition, I jotted down the name of a speaker, time of speaking, and his/her main points. This strategy was useful because, in the process of the group interview, some students were so eager to speak up that they jumped into debates without reporting their names in advance. These strategies proved efficient.

The interviews were fully and literally transcribed and then translated into English. For the purposes of data management and analysis, I transcribed the two individual interviews with the same participant in one transcription, considering them as an integral statement. Ultimately, a total of 41 transcriptions of individual interviews, plus 4 transcriptions of group interviews were generated. For the purpose of writing about this work, I then translated all the interviews into English. Two principles guided the translating: keeping most of the linguistic characteristics of each interviewee and conveying the genuine meaning of what was said.

After translating one interview into English, I invited a native Chinese speaker who also speaks fluent English to translate the English version back into Chinese and compare it with the original Chinese version. We generally agreed that the English version of the interview conveyed the same information as the Chinese version, although there were a few places where we disagreed. I modified the original translations based on our discussion. In order to translate key terms and phrases consistently, two measures were employed. I first translated four interviews (one from each grade) to identify terms and phrases frequently appearing in participants' narratives. Then a Chinese-English glossary of key terms and phrases was established and expanded throughout the process of translating the remaining interviews. The coding and analysis (which will be addressed later) was conducted on the English translations.

In the process of administering the questionnaire and interviews, I also gathered copies of documents pertaining to moral education, evaluation, and rewarding systems. These documents fell into three categories:

1. Students' written papers that recorded their own, peers', or other public figures' good deeds and/or not taking credit for doing good deeds.
2. Class records of students' awards and good deeds, including (a) Daily Class Records of Good Boys/Girls and Good Deeds (*Banji Richang Haoren Haoshi Jilu*); (b) Working Notes of Class Advisors (*Banzhuren Gongzuo Jilu*); and (c) Class Meeting Minutes (*Banhui Jilu*).
3. Policy documents issued by local educational authorities and school administration, including (a) Regulations of Moral Education for Elementary and Secondary School Students of Beijing (*Beijingshi Zhongxiaoxuesheng Deyu Tiaoli*); (b) Principles and Regulations of Character Assessment for Elementary and Secondary School Students of Beijing (*Beijingshi Zhongxiaoxuesheng Caoxing Pingding Xize*); (c) Regulations of Rewarding and Penalty for Elementary and Secondary School Students of Beijing (*Beijingshi Zhongxiaoxuesheng Jiangcheng Tiaoli*); and (d) Elementary Students' Comprehensive Evaluation Pamphlet (*Xiaoxuesheng Zhiliang Zonghe Pingjia Shouce*).

These documents were used to complement the individual interviews and data analysis. For instance, in the process of conducting the interviews, I often pointed to some of the required items in the above-mentioned "Elementary Students' Comprehensive Evaluation Pamphlet," asking the students how such evaluations were carried out, how they affected their performances, why some items were blank, or why their teachers did not fill in certain blanks.

In addition, I observed school and class activities and talked with school leaders and teachers on topics of interest. I took field notes to record what was observed on the information booth, and wall bulletin board as well as what was heard about the schools, their ecology, history, legends, and students' school life in and out of the classroom.

DATA CODING AND ANALYSIS

Questionnaire data. The questionnaire data were coded and analyzed for three purposes, as previously mentioned: (a) facilitating the selection of focal participants; (b) aiding in the design of the interview protocols; and (c) informing my overarching research questions.

In coding the questionnaires, I first removed respondents' personal information (i.e., the cover page of the questionnaire). Each questionnaire was assigned an ID number starting with respondent's grade level. The questionnaires were numbered in the order received. All the answers in the questionnaire were quantified through coding. Questions with only two possible answers (e.g., Yes vs. No; True vs. False; Agree vs. Disagree; Male vs. Female) were coded using 0 or 1. Questions with three answers (e.g., Bad, No idea, and Good; No, No idea, and Yes) were coded using -1, 0, and 1, respectively. Coded data were entered into Excel spreadsheets for analysis.

Data analysis involved counting the number (or frequency) and computing the percentage of respondents who gave positive answers to an item. In examining the frequency distribution and percentage of respondents to a certain item, I first looked for overall trends featuring youngsters' encountering and moral statements of various attitudes and practices around reporting good deeds. The differences of these trends among different age groups were then analyzed. *T*-test and *p* values were applied to determine the significance of these differences.

Interview data. Interviews provided the major data for this study. Analysis of interview data was focused on answering the guiding research questions. In the strictest sense, the coding and analysis of interview data were essentially an ongoing process that started upon the completion of the first interview and did not stop until the completion of the whole study.

The coding first involved developing a start list of codes. To this end, I randomly selected four transcriptions of individual interviews, one from each grade, and looked at each by marking the text where I believed it was interesting and offered something toward answering the overarching research questions (Seidman, 1998, p. 100). I then looked for repetition in language (words, phrases, or other meaningful units), situations, questions, and problems to recognize what might amount to meaningful trends. In so doing, four initial themes emerged (see Table 4), including "obedience to authoritative moral sources" (AUTH-MOR), "conforming to the rules of right conduct" (CONF-RUL), "considering the social consequences within a relational network with peers" (SOC-CONS), and "satisfying personal feelings" (SAT-PERF).

Table 4

Initial Codes &Themes and Their Modifications

Code		Theme	
Initial Code	Modified	Initial Theme	Modified
AUTH-MOR	AUTH	Obedience to *authoritative* moral sources	Authoritative
CONF-RUL	RULE	Conforming to the *rules* of right conduct	Rule-governed
SOC-CONS	CONS	Considering the *social consequences* within a relational network with peers	Social-consequential
SAT-PERF	EXPR	Satisfying *personal feelings*	Expressive

At this moment, I was a little uncertain if the initial conceptualization of these themes was solid enough. I decided to search through the existing literature to determine whether any well-established conceptual framework could fit well with the initial themes. This search eventually focused on Tipton's (1982, 2002) four styles of ethical discourse, each of which I found to be concisely abstracted, highly differentiated, and systematically integrated, ultimately fitting very well with the gist of each of the initial themes.

Based on Tipton's (1982, 2002) categories, I modified my initial codes and themes—obedience to *authoritative* moral sources, conforming to the *rules* of right conduct, considering the *social consequences* within a relational network with peers, and satisfying personal *feelings*—respectively as the authoritative style (AUTH), the rule-governed style (RULE), the social-consequential style (CONS),[14] and the expressive style (EXPR). I then tried the codes out, coding the four selected transcriptions, paying attention to any other potential themes, and noting supportive quotes for each style. I closely examined the supportive quotes so as to give an operational definition to each code and explicate the relationships among different codes. These efforts brought about a tentative start list of codes, entailing codes and their definitions while suggesting the relationships between different codes. To solidify the code list, I re-coded the four selected transcriptions, adding new codes while tweaking or removing some old codes.

To test the reliability of the codes, I invited a research assistant to be a second coder. After being introduced to the codes, their definitions, and the relationships among different codes, she independently coded on clean copies of the four selected transcriptions that I had already coded. I subsequently calculated the inter-rater reliability, which was high (up to 95% on average). We did have some disagreements with the expressive style; however, even in this category, the inter-rater agreement was greater than 90%. After discussing about the disagreements with her, I modified some codes and constructed a start list of codes. Aided by this start list of codes, I coded all the interview transcriptions. In coding the interviews (individual and group), I assigned each interviewee the same ID as their questionnaire ID while creating a pseudonym for each of them.

---

[14] I realize that there seem to be some overlaps between the social consequential style and the authoritative style in terms of social consequence, as the social interactions between children and adults to some extent also bring about social consequences. To avoid confusion, I would like to stress that the social consequences in this book are specifically confined to those resulting from social interactions between children and their peers.

The start list of codes was also applied to coding the group interview data, which in nature complemented, extended, and triangulated individual interview data.

The analysis of interview data involved four major steps. First of all, coded transcriptions were split into "coded segments" (Miles & Huberman, 1984). Each segment, marked with its code and the participant's ID number, was then filed into an organizer of the category to which the coded segment belongs. I closely examined the coded segments of each category and underlined key words, phrases, and/or sentences.

Next, the key words, phrases, or sentences were entered into what Miles and Huberman (1984) called a "Conceptually Clustered Matrix." The first column of the matrix lists informants' IDs while other columns are arranged to bring together the key words, phrases, or sentences that belong to a certain category. One salient advantage of a conceptually clustered matrix is that reading down the columns enables analytical comparisons among different informants and age groups while reading across the columns enables analytical comparisons among different categories (Miles & Huberman, 1984, pp. 110-111). The same strategy was used to construct a "Conceptually Clustered Matrix" for each of the four styles and further analyze specific features or discourse forms of each style.

Data entered into conceptually clustered matrixes were further analyzed. I first computed the number and percentage of informants who reported a certain category at two levels: overall and age group. Next, I conducted both overall comparisons among different categories to help identify general features of children's ethical discourse and age-group comparisons among different categories to help identify the age trajectory of each theme in children's ethical discourse.

Finally, I analyzed the relationships among salient styles of children's ethical discourse in order to create concept maps (Maxwell, 1996; Strauss & Corbin, 1998) to depict the relationships among salient styles. This analysis was conducted by closely examining informants' story narratives. In this book, I cited individual participants' narratives about reporting good deeds—how they encountered and made meanings of others' attitudes and practices around reporting good deeds as well as how they conceived their own attitudes and practices—to further explicate and exemplify the relationships among salient styles of children's ethical discourse.

In addition, I employed some complementary techniques to help with the analysis of interview data. First, I crafted narrative profiles of participants' recollections of and reflections on their experiences concerning lying about good deeds. At this stage, my role was "to read the subject's answers without prejudice and to thematize the statements from [his or]her viewpoint as understood by the researcher" (Kvale, 1996, p. 194). I also wrote analytical memos to record my emerging interpretations and stimulate analytical insights (Maxwell, 1996; Strauss & Corbin, 1998).

Supplemental data. The policy documents, class records, students' written papers, and field notes were all analyzed mainly to confirm my inferences of the socio-cultural-psychological causes for children's constructed meanings as well as to inform the cultural interpretations of children's ethical arguments for lying about good deeds. Specifically, the analysis varied based on different materials. The policy documents were read through; places pertaining to my research questions or informing my analysis of the interview data were marked. All those marked places were re-read thoroughly, and contents were sorted out in terms of (a) how schools and class advisors were required to record, report, and reward *haoren haoshi* (literally, good person good deed) and (b) what curricular and extra-curricular activities were to be organized to promote students' awareness of "not taking credit for doing good deeds." Class records and students' written papers were also read through, mainly to triangulate the stories that focal participants reported to me. In addition, the field notes were frequently read through and used to remind me of my original thoughts about, for example, a conversation with a teacher or student, a poster on the wall of the teaching building, or a story told by a focal participant.

VALIDITY ISSUES

There seems to be at least two validity threats pertaining to this research study. One has to do with the influence of my identity on the participants. It was anticipated that Chinese youngsters might regard me, a researcher from Harvard University, as an expert, which could lead them to choose to say what they think I want to know. To cope with this validity threat, known as reactivity (Maxwell, 1996), I always reassured the participants at the very beginning of each interview that there were no right or wrong answers to any of my interview questions. Nevertheless, some interviewees frequently asked whether they correctly answered the questions, and others usually gave ambiguous answers to the questions, saying that such and such is both right and wrong while at the same time looking into my eyes as if trying to read my mind or figure out how their answers might be right. In such situations, I reassured them that the goal of the interview was not to evaluate whether their answers were right or wrong, but to understand why certain attitudes or practices around reporting good deeds mattered to them or not. This effort proved effective as students' answers became increasingly specific and articulate.

The other validity threat has to do with the influence of my potential bias on data interpretation. I was born, grew up, and educated in mainland China. My socialization experiences shaped many (but definitely not all) of my social, cultural, conventional, and moral beliefs. To deal with the plausible threat of researcher bias to the interpretation of the data, I have tried my best not to impose my own beliefs on understanding participants' narratives. I have also triangulated data interpretation by frequently checking with my research colleagues (Denzin, 1978). In addition, I really wanted to learn about the phenomenon I was studying, so I had little motivation to influence what I was finding. I believe that distance usually enables people to see things more clearly and from different perspectives. After almost eight years of living, studying, and working in the United States, I have learned how to maintain a distance between my analytical turn of mind and the objects to be analyzed.

CHAPTER 3
Descriptive Statistics of Chinese Children's Ethical Discourse

Saints should always be judged guilty until they are proved innocent, but the tests that have to be applied to them are not, of course, the same in all cases.

—George Orwell (1961)

Children told stories about their lived experiences related to conducting good deeds and not taking credit for them and reflected back upon the meanings they made of such experiences. They also made ethical statements on the moral goodness and obligation of lying about good deeds. Differences in Chinese children's attitudes and practices related to reporting good deeds were fundamentally rooted in variations in children's ethical discourse within four ideal styles: authoritative, rule-governed, social consequential, and expressive.

STORY NARRATIVES

STORIES OF GOOD DEEDS

Chinese children's ethical discourse was expressed and represented in their story narratives. Table 5 presents the major categories of the story narratives of good deeds. Overall, the focal participants (n = 41) told 175 stories about doing good deeds, including 32 stories (18%) told by second graders (n = 11), 45 (26%) by fourth graders (n = 8), 53 (30%) by sixth graders (n = 12), and 45 (26%) by ninth graders (n = 10).

Table 5

Features of Story Narratives about Good Deeds

Doer of Deed		Number of Good Deeds Reported by Grade								Total	(%)
		2nd		4th		6th		9th			
SELF	(%)	11	(15%)	21	(29%)	24	(33%)	16	(22%)	72	(41%)
PEER	(%)	12	(20%)	14	(23%)	17	(28%)	17	(28%)	60	(34%)
ROM	(%)	9	(21%)	10	(23%)	12	(28%)	12	(28%)	43	(25%)
Total	(%)	32	(18%)	45	(26%)	53	(30 %)	45	(26%)	175	(100%)

Note: SELF = reporting participants themselves; PEER = peer students or friends; ROM = role models.

In terms of who the doer of a good deed is, these 175 good deeds fall into three general categories. One category (SELF) includes 72 deeds (41%) conducted by the reporting participants themselves. These SELF deeds mostly involve either helping people (e.g., schoolmates, strangers in the streets, and neighbors in one's residential area) or serving institutions (e.g., residential communities, schools).

Another category (PEER) includes 60 deeds (34%) witnessed or heard by the reporting participants but conducted by their peer students or friends. These PEER deeds also involve either helping someone or serving some institution and thus are in nature similar to the SELF deeds. In the words of the focal participants, the good deeds of both categories are mostly "small deeds that most people can do under similar circumstances."

The third category (ROM) includes 43 deeds (25%) conducted by role models as propagated by all kinds of media, such as radio, TV, movies, newspapers, magazines, and books. These ROM stories are generally what the focal participants called "big deeds, which not anyone can have the opportunity or courage to do."

One such ROM story repeatedly reported by all ninth-grade focal participants (n = 10) was about a role model named Tangning, who in the 1960s was attending their alma mater Font High School. Tangning saved a drowning girl from a frozen lake in Font Commons at the cost of his own life. Tangning has since been remembered by his alma mater and its generations of schoolmates. Font High School has even set up a merit-based scholarship in his name, known as Tangning Scholarship, which is awarded to approximately 10 students every academic year for their excellence in academic achievements, leadership, or service.

STORIES OF LYING ABOUT GOOD DEEDS

Table 6 presents the general categories of stories pertaining to "not taking credit for doing good deeds." Of all the 175 good deeds reported by students in the focal sample, 75 deeds (43%) had never been told to their teachers, who requested or invited the students to report their good deeds. These 75 unpublicized good deeds include 11 deeds (15%) reported by second graders, 16 (21%) by fourth graders, 27 (36%) by sixth graders, and 21 (28%) by ninth graders.

However, most of these unpublicized good deeds were conducted by the reporting participants themselves. Specifically, 55 (73.3%) of the unpublicized good deeds belong to the SELF category. For instance, a second grader reported that he went to a public park every Saturday morning to collect "white trash" (e.g., plastic bags, bottles) scattered throughout the park. He did not tell anyone about this, even when his teacher asked the class to report their good deeds for evaluative purposes.

Table 6

Stories of Lying about Good Deeds

Doer of Deed		Number of Unpublicized Good Deeds by Grade				Total (%)
		2nd	4th	6th	9th	
SELF	(%)	8 (15%)	11 (20%)	20 (36%)	16 (29%)	55 (73.3%)
PEER	(%)	3 (16%)	5 (26%)	7 (37%)	4 (21%)	19 (25.3%)
ROM	(%)	0	0	0	1 (100%)	1 (1.3%)
Total	(%)	11(15%)	16 (21%)	27 (36%)	21 (28%)	75 (100%)

Approximately a quarter (19 deeds) of the unpublicized good deeds falls into the PEER category. For example, a fourth grader reported that a friend of hers helped the community remove unauthorized commercial postings from public buildings, traffic light poles, and bus stops. She happened to witness her friend's deed, but her friend did not report it when the teacher asked the class to report their good deeds for evaluative purposes.

In addition, only one of the unpublicized good deeds belongs to the ROM category. According to a ninth grader's report, a TV program named "Prides of

China" (*zhongguo jiaoao*) introduces "little guys" (*xiao renwu*) who help people in danger or urgent need but leave quietly or do not leave their name when requested. Moreover, three students[15] talked about a TV program that reported about a young worker who helped approximately 30 passengers get out of a damaged bus after a traffic accident. When some of the rescued passengers asked the young worker to leave his name and contact information, he left quietly; no one knew who he was or where to find him. To be sure, the young worker was ultimately "dug out" because one of the rescued passengers called her family using the young worker's cell phone and thus was able to find the young worker, who was subsequently honored as one of the "Figures Moving China" (*gandong zhongguo renwu*) for "doing good deeds without leaving their names."

ETHICAL STATEMENTS

Participants made a total of 454 ethical statements about the moral goodness or obligation of not taking credit for doing good deeds or "doing good deeds without leaving one's name." Table 7 presents the descriptive statistics on these ethical statements, which—as we can see—fall into four general categories, each of which suggests a distinctive ethical orientation.

Four Orientations

Of the 454 ethical statements, 51 (11%) suggest a strong authoritative ethical orientation (AUTH) for their strong sensitivity to the attitudes and/or responses of authority. For example, Mengjie, a second grader, explained why she

[15] Even though this story was told by three students, it was only counted once.

believed that it was good that she did not tell her good deed to her teacher even under request, stating that, "I feared that the teacher would criticize me."

Second, 72 (16%) of the ethical statements show strong orientation of conformism to traditional socio-moral rules of right conduct around reporting good deeds and suggest a rule-governed ethical orientation (RULE). For instance, Xueyue, a fourth grader, explained why he did not share about his good deed, saying that, "One is expected to be modest (*qianxu*)."

Third, 237 (52%) of the ethical statements expressed confident negative expectations regarding what would happen to one's public image among or interpersonal relationships with peer students as a result of taking credit for one's good deeds, suggesting a strong social consequential orientation (CONS). Sixth grader Lina's words provide a good example: "People basically just feel that they just want their classmates (rather than their teacher) to have good judgments about them. So they don't tell the teacher their good deeds in case their classmates will be unhappy."

Table 7

Features of Chinese Children's Ethical Statements

General Orientation	Number (%) of Ethical Statements By Grade				Total (%)
	2nd	4th	6th	9th	
AUTH (%)	18 (35%)	4 (8%)	17 (33%)	12 (24%)	51 (11%)
RULE (%)	2 (3%)	17 (24%)	26 (36%)	27 (38%)	72 (16%)
CONS (%)	11 (5%)	48 (20%)	69 (29%)	109 (46%)	237 (52%)
EXPR (%)	7 (7%)	16 (17%)	39 (42%)	32 (34%)	94 (21%)
Total (%)	38 (8%)	94 (21%)	151 (33%)	180 (40%)	454(100%)

Note: AUTH = authoritative; RULE = rule-governed; CONS = social consequential; EXPR = expressive.

The fourth category, which accounted for 94 (21%) of the ethical statements, suggests a strong expressive ethical orientation (EXPR), attending to the qualities of personal feelings (e.g., emotions, sentiments, and desires) in arguing against truth-telling about good deeds. For instance, Yawen, a ninth grader, explained her reasoning for not telling her teacher about her good deed: "Doing a good deed makes you feel happy about yourself. Then, why bother to tell others?"

INTEGRAL MULTIPLICITIES

Although these ethical statements overall suggest four distinctive ethical orientations, any one child's ethical statements are not necessarily confined to a single ethical orientation, but appear to be characteristic of integral multiplicities. In other words, one child's ethical statements suggest more than one ethical orientation, including both a predominant orientation that appears most frequently and other minor orientations occasionally appearing in his or her ethical statements. The predominant ethical orientation, along with other minor ethical orientations, constitutes an integral entity of one's ethical discourse.

Songou, a ninth grader attending Font High School, argued for his decision not to tell the truth about his good deed using a total of 32 ethical statements. Of them, 26 (81%) expressed confident negative expectations for social consequences of threat to his public image among peer students, 3 suggested a strong orientation toward responses of authority, 2 toward traditional socio-moral rules, and 1 toward how personal feelings might be hurt due to truth-telling about good deeds. As can be seen, Songou's ethical statements indicate a multiple-orientation character, including a predominant ethical orientation toward considering social consequences and other minor ethical orientations as well.

Table 8 presents the descriptive statistics on the integral multiplicities of Chinese children's ethical statements. Of the 41 students, only 7 (17%) students made mono-oriented ethical statements, including 5 second graders, 1 fourth grader, and 1 sixth grader. The other 34 (83%) students made dual-, triple-, or quadruple-oriented ethical statements, always with one orientation taking precedence over others. Specifically, 10 (24.4%) focal participants made dual-oriented ethical statements, 12 (29.3%) made triple-oriented ethical statements, and another 12 (29.3%) made quad-oriented ethical statements.

Table 8

Multiple-Orientations of Chinese Children's Ethical Statements

Grade	n	No. (%) of Mono-Oriented Ss	Number (%) of Multiple-Oriented Ss		
			Dual-Oriented	Triple-Oriented	Quad-Oriented
2nd	11	5 (46%)	4 (36%)	2 (18%)	0
4th	08	1 (13%)	2 (25%)	3 (38%)	2 (25%)
6th	12	1 (8%)	1 (8%)	4 (33%)	6 (50%)
9th	10	0	3 (30%)	3 (30%)	4 (40%)
			10 (24.4%)	12 (29.3%)	12 (29.3%)
Total	41	7 (17%)	34 (83%)		

The integral multiplicities characteristic of children's ethical orientation as expressed in their ethical statements appear to vary with different age groups. As Table 9 illustrates, 6 (55%) of the second graders (n = 11), 7 (88%) of the fourth graders (n = 8), 11 (92%) of the sixth graders (n = 12), and 10 (100%) of the ninth graders (n = 10) made multiple-oriented statements. It seems that, as age increases, children tend to make more complex, multiple-oriented ethical statements. However, considering the small sample size and the lack of rigorous statistical testing, we should interpret this result with caution.

ETHICAL DISCOURSE

FOUR STYLES

According to the conceptual framework previously discussed in this book and the predominant ethical orientation as suggested in individuals' ethical statements, a child was assigned to one of the four major styles of ethical discourse: the authoritative style (AUTH), the rule-governed style (RULE), the social consequential style (CONS), or the expressive style (EXPR). Each style is named after its predominant ethical orientation as expressed and represented in the child's ethical statements.

Specifically, Chinese children who hold to the authoritative style of ethical discourse are those who appear to have a strong orientation toward the attitudes and/or responses of authority figures (e.g., family members and school teachers) when reporting good deeds. Children assigned to the rule-governed style include those whose ethical statements are strongly oriented toward the rules or principles of right conduct (e.g., honesty and humility) that have long been highlighted in Chinese society. The social consequential style, in the sense of social interactions between a child and his or her peers, is mainly oriented toward the social or interpersonal consequences of reporting good deeds (e.g., loss of friendship, disharmony of peer relationships, or peers' negative evaluation). Finally, the expressive style is mainly oriented toward the qualities of personal feelings (e.g., embarrassment, happiness, fear, or self-satisfaction); for a child whose ethical discourse suggests an expressive style, personal emotions, sentiments, and desires are among those that drive him or her to avoid truth-telling about his or her good deed because he or she believes that it is bad to tell the truth about good deeds in general.

FREQUENCY DISTRIBUTION OF THE FOUR STYLES

The four styles of Chinese children's ethical discourse could be arranged in a hierarchical order or sequence according to the number (percentage) of the children whose ethical statements indicate a certain style of ethical discourse. This sequence starts with the social consequential style, followed by the authoritative style, expressive style, and rule-governed style.

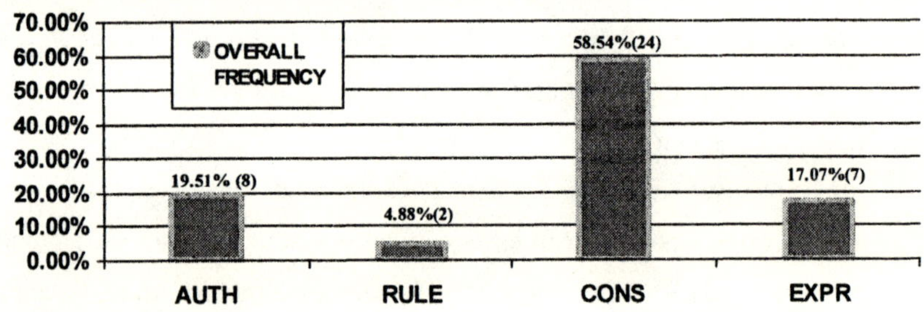

Figure 3. Frequency Distribution of Ethical Discourse by Style.
AUTH = authoritative; RULE = rule-governed; CONS = social consequential; EXPR = expressive

As indicated in Figure 3, the social consequential style (CONS) has the most reporters, with a commanding majority or 24 students (58.54%) of the focal sample (n = 41) making ethical statements that are predominantly oriented toward one's confident negative expectations of peer students' responses to reporting good deeds. In other words, the orientation toward social consequences is outstanding in Chinese children's ethical statements on the moral goodness and obligation of lying about one's good deeds. The predominance of the social consequential style seems consistent with what the current literature (e.g., Blum, 2007) has suggested about the role of considering social consequences in Chinese socio-moral reasoning.

The authoritative style (AUTH) ranks second, including 8 students (19.51%) of the focal sample whose ethical statements suggest a predominant ethical orientation toward the responses of authority. Third is the expressive style (EXPR), with 7 students (17.07%) of the focal sample reporting a predominant ethical orientation toward the qualities of personal feelings as experienced in their decision-making about whether to lie or tell the truth about a good deed. Noteworthy is that the frequency difference between the authoritative style (19.51%) and the expressive style (17.07%) is not significant. The rule-governed style (RULE) rates last; only 2 students (4.88%) of the focal sample expressed a predominant orientation toward traditional socio-moral rules of right conduct, such as modesty or humility.

This comparison of the overall frequency distribution of the four ethical discourse styles seems to suggest that, in justifying attitudes and practices of lie- or truth-telling about a good deed, very few of the Chinese children in the focal sample attend to the socio-moral rules of right conduct. Instead, the majority turn to factors such as social consequences of threats to peer relationships, responses of authority, and personal feelings. This finding reveals to some degree that it is necessary to reconsider what has been suggested in the existing literature (e.g., Lee et al., 1997, 2001; Fu et al., 2001), which almost without exception attributed Chinese children's attitudes and practices of lying about good deeds to their conforming to the traditional Chinese socio-moral rules of right conduct, such as modesty or humility.

AGE DIFFERENCE IN ETHICAL DISCOURSE

Overall, the status of a discourse style varies based on age groups. As Figure 4 indicates, the authoritative style dominated the ethical discourse of the second graders, while the consequential style dominated that of the fourth, sixth, and ninth graders. This seems to suggest that, in considering the moral goodness or behavioral obligation of lying about good deeds, second graders are highly sensitive to the attitudes or responses of their parents and school teachers. In contrast, fourth, sixth, and ninth graders tend to give greater weight to the attitudes and/or responses of peer students or friends. In other words, these older children seem to have come to realize the significance of peer students' and friends' attitudes and responses in helping them maintain positive public image and interpersonal harmony.

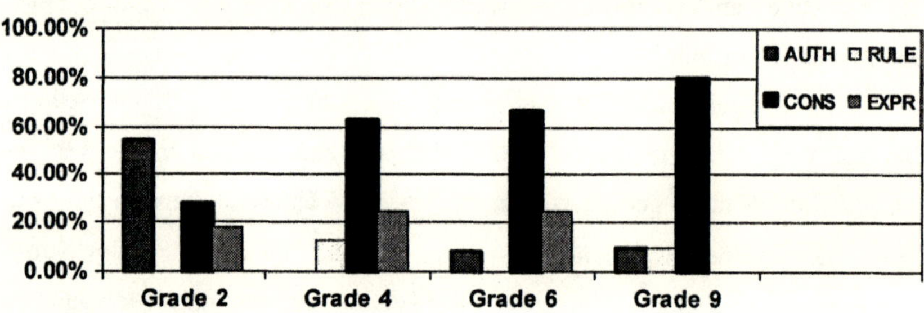

Figure 4. Frequency Distribution of Ethical Discourse by Age Group

Second graders. The authoritative style dominates second graders' ethical discourse. As Table 9 shows, 6 (54.55%) of the second graders (n = 11) reported a strong orientation toward the responses of such authority figures as family members and school teachers. For these students, being a good child in the eyes of school teachers and parents or grandparents takes precedence over other considerations. The social consequential style which ranks first overall (as shown in Figure 3) ranks second among this group, with 3 (27.27%) of the second graders reporting confident negative expectations regarding the way peer students and friends would respond to truth-telling about good deeds.

The expressive style ranks third, with 2 (18.18%) of the second graders reporting confident expectations regarding the qualities of personal feelings in emotional experiences. The rule-governed style ranks fourth; none of the second graders hold to the rule-governed style. While I did find that 2 second graders made rule-oriented ethical statements, neither was dominated by the rule-governed orientation. This seems to suggest that the second graders may be at the very beginning of learning about socio-moral rules of right conduct such as humility or modesty, but they have yet to internalize these rules into their ethical discourse.

Table 9

Frequency Distribution of Ethical Discourse by Style and Age Group

Styles	Number (%) of Students of Each Style by Grade (n)				Total (41)
	2nd (11)	4th (8)	6th (12)	9th (10)	
AUTH	6 (54.55%)	0	1 (8.33%)	1(10.00%)	8 (19.51%)
RULE	0	1 (12.50%)	0	1(10.00%)	2 (04.88%)
CONS	3 (27.27%)	5 (62.50%)	8 (66.67%)	8(80.00%)	24 (58.54%)
EXPR	2 (18.18%)	2 (25.00%)	3 (25.00%)	0	7 (17.07%)

Fourth graders. The social consequential style dominates fourth graders' ethical discourse. To be specific, 5 (62.50%) of them (n = 8) reported a strong orientation toward confident negative expectations for the responses of peer students or friends to truth-telling about good deeds. For these students, developing and maintaining friendship and good interpersonal relationships appear to be more important than other considerations. The expressive style ranks second; 2 (25.00%) of the fourth graders reported a dominant orientation toward the qualities of personal feelings as expected to be experienced around reporting good deeds.

The rule-governed style ranks third, with just 1 (12.50%) of the 8 fourth graders reporting a dominant orientation toward considering rules of right conduct as prescribed by the Chinese culture. The authoritative style ranks fourth; none of the 8 fourth graders revealed a dominant orientation toward the attitudes and/or responses of authority. Although I did find that 3 fourth graders made authoritative ethical statements, none was dominated by confident expectations for the responses of family members, teachers, or other significant authority figures.

Sixth graders. The social consequential style dominates sixth graders' ethical discourse. Specifically, 8 students (66.67%) of this group (n = 12) expressed a predominant orientation toward confident negative expectations for the attitudes and responses of peer students or friends to truth-telling about good deeds. For these children, how peer students and friends look at and get along with them exerts a commanding influence on their own attitudes and behavioral choices in the situation of lie- or truth-telling about good deeds. The expressive style ranks second; 3 (25%) of the sixth graders indicated a predominant orientation toward considering the qualities of personal feelings that might be experienced in reporting good deeds.

The authoritative style ranks third, with only 1 (8.33%) of the sixth graders demonstrating a predominant orientation toward the attitudes and/responses of their parents or school teachers. In fourth place is the rule-governed style; none of the sixth graders shows a predominant orientation toward the socio-moral rules of right conduct, such as humility or modesty. It is true that 8 (66.67%) of the sixth graders made rule-governed ethical statements, but these statements were in large measure overshadowed by their predominant consequential, expressive, or authoritative ethical statements.

It can be inferred that the sixth graders have generally acquired some knowledge about the socio-moral rules of correct behavior. However, as relational beings, they have also come to realize that—within a relational network—other factors are more important than conforming to traditional socio-moral rules. Moreover, this realization seems to have been strengthened by their increased social experience.

Ninth graders. The social consequential style also dominates ninth graders' ethical discourse, with 8 (80%) of this group (n = 10) indicating a predominant orientation toward confident negative expectations for the attitudes and responses of peer students or friends to truth-telling about good deeds. For these students, positive public image and harmonious interpersonal relationships are far more important than other considerations, such as teachers' responses and traditional socio-moral rules.

The rule-governed style and authoritative style tie in terms of the number (percentage) of students showing predominant orientations. Specifically, only 1 (10%) ninth grader indicated a predominant rule-governed orientation while another 1 (10%) indicated a predominant authoritative orientation. It is noteworthy that the only ninth grader who holds to the rule-governed discourse style made 13 rule-oriented ethical statements, 10 social consequential ethical statements, and 9 expressive ethical statements. In comparison, the only ninth grader holding to the authoritative style made just one statement suggesting obvious authoritative orientation and another statement of vague rule-governed orientation.

In fourth place is the expressive style; none of the ninth graders showed a predominant orientation toward the qualities of personal feelings around reporting good deeds. To be sure, 8 (80%) of the ninth graders made ethical statements indicating expressive elements, but none were dominated by personal feelings. It seems that the ninth graders become very practical and rational when facing moral dilemmas; for them, priority is given to the maintenance of a positive public image, interpersonal harmony, and a healthy social network.

CHAPTER 4
Four Styles of Chinese Children's Ethical Discourse

Lies are often much more plausible, more appealing to reason, than reality, since the liar has the great advantage of knowing beforehand what the audience wishes or expects to hear.

—Hannah Arendt (1972)

THE AUTHORITATIVE STYLE

This study has found that Chinese children take into account authoritative sources (both social and family) when considering the moral goodness or obligation of lying about good deeds. Social authority, as used in this study, refers to children's schoolteachers while family authority refers to their parents. Of the 8 students (including 6 second graders, 1 sixth grader, and 1 ninth grader) who hold to the authoritative style, only the sixth grader gave priority to the attitudes and/or responses of parents. The remaining 7 students of the authoritative style considered factors with respect to their schoolteachers.

A closer examination of these children's specific ethical statements also suggests the same tendency: Schoolteachers are far more frequently referred to as authoritative sources than parents in regard to children's moral and ethical decisions. These 8 children made a total of 51 authoritative ethical statements. Among these, a commanding majority—namely, 48 statements (94.12%)—was concentrated on factors with respect to teachers' attitudes and/or responses. Only 5.88 percent (3 statements) focused on parents' attitudes and/or responses. This difference might be associated to some extent with the nature of lying about good deeds, which, as a social phenomenon, primarily occurs in school settings. As suggested in children's story narratives, in family settings, children's self-reporting of good deeds occurs with little trepidation of how parents may respond to reporting good deeds. However, in school settings, one's behaviors—such as truth-telling about good deeds—may have high stakes.

TEACHER AS AUTHORITY

The importance of teachers for school children can hardly be overstated. This also holds true in the case of lying about good deeds. Factors with regard to teachers are most frequently referred to as authoritative sources in Chinese children's ethical statements about why it is good or obligatory to lie about one's good deeds. These factors roughly fall into four general categories: (a) interest, (b) distrust, (c) criticism, and (d) distance.

Interest. This category has to do with children's speculations about whether or not their teachers are really interested in knowing about their good deeds. Teachers' interest matters, especially for the second and sixth graders, as indicated in their ethical statements, which offer insights into their inner voices. Children—upon request—were reluctant to report their good deeds mainly because they thought that the teachers who asked students to report good deeds were not really interested in their good deeds.

What should be noted is that, although the students provided some descriptions of how their teachers responded to their classmates' good deed reporting, they did not provide in-depth explanation regarding why they so interpreted their teachers' intention. From the experience of a cultural "insider," I suspect that children believed so mainly because teachers did not reward students as much as they expected for doing good deeds. Other explanations are possible. For example, some teachers might truly have no real interest in knowing about their students' good deeds. They may ask students to report good deeds simply because they want to show that they are doing the job a teacher is supposed to do. Perhaps, for these teachers themselves, it has little meaning whether or not their students conducted good deeds and what they did. This is an area worthy of further research.

Children in the focal sample seem to have acquired some practical wisdom from observing the way their teachers handled their reported good deeds. They observed that, although teachers occasionally asked students to report their good deeds during their weekly class meetings, teachers had never recorded students' reported good deeds in the Primary School Students' Comprehensive Evaluation Pamphlet *(xiaoxuesheng zhiliang zonghe pingjia shouce*). Every student had a copy of that pamphlet, which their teachers should fill out; but all the pamphlets of the focal participants were found to be blank, even at the end of the semester.

This may be, as some may speculate, because no students have ever done any good deeds. However, the truth is that a good many students interviewed said that they themselves or their classmates indeed perform deeds, some of which had already been reported or publicized. When asked what was going on, students simply shrugged it off, saying that their teachers had never recorded their performance in the pamphlets. Students thus came to believe that teachers were actually "doing face-work"—pretending to be interested in knowing about students' good deeds but in fact having little genuine interest in their deeds.

These children seem to have also learned some lessons from observing fellow students' experiences. In the young eyes of the students, peer students' experiences teach the lessons whereby they would decide their own choice of action. Wenyan, a second grade girl, was an active talker and always eager to express her ideas. She recalled that, when her classmates reported their good deeds as required by their head teacher, "the head teacher just smiled it away (*heheyixiao*)" without giving any other signals of approval or disapproval.

What's more, children have grasped important lessons from their personal lived experiences. Wenyan recalled her experience when she volunteered to clean up the classroom. When her teacher asked who mopped the floor, she told the truth and answered that it was she. However, the head teacher did not give any encouraging response except to say "uh huh." Wenyan thus thought that her teacher was not really interested in what had happened at all.

Wenyan's peer students agreed her interpretation. For instance, Shijie (2M[16]) stated that, even if one reported one's good deeds, "the head teacher won't say anything or at most gives you a smile or a few words of praise." Xuhan (2M) remarked that "even if I tell [the truth about my good deeds], there is little meaning, except for a few words of praise [...] the teacher just wants to show she is doing her job, that is it."

To be sure, the second graders were not the only group who believed that teachers were doing face-work rather than really being interested in knowing about students' good deeds. Yangyong (6M) recalled his own experience:

> [Telling the truth of your good deeds] is no use. At most the teacher will give you a cheap smile or a few words of praise...The teacher might just say a few words of praise. That is it. After a few seconds or minutes, it is over...The teacher might just say "ah ha"... [so I] would not tell, as even if you told the truth, at most you got a smile...a few words of praise. There is nothing more to happen. The teacher does not really want to know about your deeds. She is just doing her job.

When asked whether what the younger participants said was true, Boyuan (9M) also recalled his own experience of receiving teacher's "cold" responses:

---

[16] This is a convenient form for conveying participants' background information. It consists of grade (i.e., 2, 4, 6, or 9) and gender (F for female; M for male). For example, Wenyan (2F) means that Wenyan is a second-grade girl, while Bida (9M) means that Bida is a ninth-grade boy.

> When I told [my good deed] to the teacher, she simply said "good job." [It seems to me that,] when the teacher got to know the deed, she just appeared as if she had known about it. That's it.

As these examples demonstrate, Chinese teachers generally responded to students' truth-telling about their good deeds with some oral approval. It is quite likely that teachers did not intend to convey what students perceived, but just did not give enough encouraging responses to the students' good deeds. However, this shortage of encouraging responses is perceived by students as their teachers simply having no real interest in their good deeds or doing face-work—namely, pretending to ask the students to report their good deeds, but having no genuine interest in what the deeds really were or what had truly happened. Students' stereotypical understanding was strengthened by their personal lived experiences and repeated observations of teachers' face-work and peers' experiences.

Distrust. The second category highlights what can be called teachers' distrust. Children expressed confident expectations that, even if they reported their good deeds as required, their teachers would not believe the truthfulness of their good deeds. They suggested that the teachers would assume that they wanted to earn something (e.g., praise) by reporting their good deeds. Students who hold to this belief were all from the sixth and ninth grades, including 4 sixth graders (one strong authoritative style and three other styles) and 5 ninth graders (one strong authoritative style and four other styles). Both sixth and ninth graders expressed confident expectations regarding their teachers' distrust, stating that their teachers would not believe the truthfulness of the good deeds but think that the students fabricated a good deed to earn something in exchange for doing good deeds that the teacher thought did not exist.

However, as indicated in their specific forms of discourse, some slight differences emerged in terms of certainty about teachers' distrust. The sixth graders without exception used an identical form of discourse with some uncertainty, such as "the teacher maybe won't…," "the teacher may not…," and "the teacher does not necessarily…." For instance, Han (6M) said, "If I tell the truth, my teacher maybe won't believe it." Wan (6F) said, "If I tell the truth to the teacher, the teacher may not believe it." Dong (6M) remarked that, if a student reported a good deed to his or her teacher, "the teacher might think that he [or she] did not simply do a good deed; instead, by doing the good deed he wanted others to know about him." Dong's speculation of teacher's distrust was echoed by his classmate Xu (6F), who recalled that her classmate Rui (6F) helped an ill senior lady to the hospital on her way to school but did not tell the truth about the good deed when their head teacher asked students to report good deeds. When asked whether Rui should have told the truth about her good deed, Xu remarked:

> I feel that it is just fine for Rui to tell the truth directly, though the teacher does not necessarily believe it even if she tells the truth, and the teacher might think that she wants to earn something. (*Interviewer: Suppose you were Rui. Would you have told the truth?*) Suppose I were Rui…let me see…suppose I were Rui, I wouldn't…anyway, I wouldn't tell the truth (Laugh). I would not tell the truth to my teacher. I wouldn't tell, because I fear that the teacher wouldn't believe me, thinking that I am fabricating it, thinking that I want to earn something.

It is interesting to see the self-vs.-other difference in Xu's discourse. She felt that she herself would not tell the truth about a good deed but it was fine for her classmate Rui to tell the truth, although she expected the teacher not to believe either Rui or herself. Even she herself immediately realized the self-vs.-other controversy, bursting into laughter. What's more, Xu expressed expectation for her teacher's distrust, but her discourse in the form of "one does not necessarily…" also suggested uncertainty. That being said, one thing is certain in the students' discourse: Their teacher would be skeptical of the truthfulness of the good deed and the students' motivation for telling the truth about a good deed (i.e., to earn something by fabricating a good deed).

The ninth graders also expressed confident expectations that their teacher would be skeptical of the truthfulness of a reported good deed and/or the motivation of the students who told the truth of their good deeds. What is different is the degree of certainty to which they expected their teachers to be skeptical. Although some ninth graders seemed to be uncertain, others appeared to be much surer about their teachers' distrust. For instance, Lixiang (9M) said, "The teacher won't necessarily believe me; she might be thinking that I fabricated a good deed to get praise." Qian (9F) used almost the same speaking tone of uncertainty, saying, "The teacher does not necessarily believe me." However, several students' discourse expressed certainty about teachers' distrust. Hua (9M) said, "If I tell the truth, the teacher would not believe me." Lixiang (9M) and Yawen (9F) used the same form of discourse: "If I tell the truth, the teacher would definitely not believe me."

It is not quite clear what caused the Chinese children to believe that their teachers might not believe them. During the interview, the focal participants—even under request—were unable to provide in-depth explanations for their belief. That being said, three tentative explanations may apply. One may have to do with the fact that most of these good deeds happened without being witnessed, which reduced the believability of the deeds. Another key may be related to Chinese teachers' tacit criteria for passing judgment. The focal participants seemed to suggest that their teachers—at least in the young eyes of the children—tended to judge the character of students based on their academic achievement or performance at school. Just as Songou (9M) stated, "The teacher won't believe you if you don't work hard at school [...and] if your academic performance is especially bad, the teacher might think: Can this student do a good deed as he [or she] has said?" Still another key, as suggested by Blum (2007) and especially Lian (1993), might relate to Chinese people's mindset of social distrust, which evolved out of its ancient civilization and was strengthened in the last several decades. Lian (1993) carries out an extensive discussion about the history and present prevalence of social distrust in China.

Criticism. The third category focuses around teachers' criticism. Chinese children in the focal sample expressed confident expectations that, if they told the truth about their good deeds, their teachers would criticize them. Indeed, all 6 second graders holding to the authoritative style suggested that their teachers might criticize them and unanimously used the same form of discourse: "The teacher would criticize or punish me." For the second graders, it seems that teachers are identified more as someone who could blame, criticize, and punish them for making mistakes and misbehaviors than someone who could be trusted with the truth of a good deed. Meanwhile, neither the only sixth grader nor the only ninth grader of the authoritative style reported potential criticism. This seems to some extent intriguing initially. Why should Chinese teachers criticize their students for reporting their good deeds? Do they criticize students for the good deeds themselves or for something else? In order to answer these questions, we have to go back to the settings in which the good deeds occurred.

A closer reading of children's story narratives reveals that, whenever a student said that he or she was afraid that the teacher would criticize him or her, it was all about good deeds that occurred off school campus and in which the students offered help to strangers. This seems to be an important revelation. To further confirm this interpretation, a post-interview discussion about this issue was conducted with Ms. Yang, moral educator and director of Pacific Primary School's Young Pioneers League. Ms. Yang said that, in order to protect the students from any potential hurt or harm, the school had long been discouraging primary school students from having contact with strangers outside of school settings. Consequently, Chinese schools—especially urban schools—have developed Safety Education (*anquan jiaoyu*) programs to increase students' safety awareness for self-defense.

Distance. The fourth category is the distance (in the sense of closeness of relationship) between student and teacher, which directly impinges students' decision-making of whether or not to tell their good deeds to their teachers. Students' awareness for relational distance was found to be age-specific. Only the sixth- and ninth-grade participants reported the role of the distance between student and teacher in their decision-making. Their discourse offered insights into their inner voices. For instance, Yawen (9F) stated:

> I make decisions based on the distance between me and my teacher, based on who the teacher is...whether the teacher...whether or not the teacher is someone with whom I am very familiar...that is, a sense of distance. In most cases, I will not tell my good deeds to the teacher who asks me to report unless I believe there is a close enough relationship between me and the teacher.

However, the reality is that most Chinese students—especially primary school students—had difficulty shortening the distance between them and their teachers. They explained that this was because students generally feared their teachers and because, in the eyes of Chinese primary school students, their teachers were symbols of discipline, criticism, and punishments rather than someone with whom they could truly stay close. A good example is what Lixiang (9M) remarked:

> You know, primary school students all fear their teachers. No matter what the teacher says to them, they might burst into tears.....When they are afraid of their teachers, they have difficulty maintaining close relationships with their teachers. Teachers in the eyes of primary school students are the symbols of criticism, punishment, and the like.

Therefore, in most cases, children would choose to keep the good deeds in their own minds even when their teachers ask them to report good deeds for evaluative purposes. Wanyu (6F) makes a good case for those children who, in making a decision as to whether or not to share their good deeds, weigh the distance between teachers and students. She first told me a story about her good deed with the following lines:

> Last year, just at the beginning of the new semester, on my way to school I saw a crowd of people gathering on the street. I thought there was something interesting, so I went over to see what's happening. Then I noticed an old lady lying on the ground, looking like she was in a very difficult condition. Nobody seemed to offer any help. I thought I had to do something. Fortunately I had a cell phone at that time, so I dialed 120 (medical emergency number). I

> waited for almost 20 minutes till an ambulance came and picked up the lady.

Later in a weekly class meeting (*banhui*), Wanyu's head teacher (*banzhuren*) asked the class to report their good deeds for evaluative purposes, but Wanyu did not report to her teacher the good deed. She later explained her decision to me with the following lines:

> There is distance between us and our head teacher. She (the head teacher) has yet to develop a close relationship with me. I don't quite know about her…I still do not know about our head teacher very well. I just won't tell my good deeds to someone I do not really know about.

As can be seen, while children would love to be positively evaluated and praised for helping others, they did not report their good deeds because they perceived distance between them and the head teacher. Notwithstanding, considering the small number of students who mentioned the distance factor, we should interpret with caution the distance between Chinese students and their teachers.

Parents as Authority

Parents in general are undoubtedly among the most important authoritative sources for youngsters' ethical decision-making. However, in the case of lying about good deeds, the attitudes and/or responses of parents as authoritative sources appear to be overshadowed by those of teachers. As previously explained, this might be due to the fact that children's lying about good deeds oftentimes happens in social or school settings rather than in family settings.

That being said, focal participants in this study still made a few statements regarding the way in which the attitudes and/or responses of parents function as authoritative sources for youngsters' ethical decision-making. Indicated in participants' ethical statements were their parents' instructions and attitudes which function as the authoritative sources for ethical decision-making.

In general, Chinese parents teach their children to be humble or modest and to be cautious of speaking in public. For the children, parents' words are an important source of moral knowledge and the criteria to which they refer when they need to make an ethical decision. For instance, Pan (6M) told me a story of his lying to his teacher about a good deed he accomplished:

> One day my friends and I originally wanted to go shopping. Just as we started to walk over a wooden bridge, we saw a waste collector pushing a tricycle to cross the bridge, but he was having difficulty. The bridge was broken, too shabby to endure a fully loaded tricycle to cross over. The waste collector was about to unload all his stuff and carry it over the bridge. So we decided to help him with it. After helping him move his stuff across the bridge, we then went shopping.

When asked why he did not share his good deed with his teacher as requested in their class meeting, Pan (6M) answered by referring to his parents' instructions:

> A: My parents always tell me not to show off/publicize my good deeds, not to distinguish myself.
> Q: Why do they say this?
> A: I don't know. Perhaps they are afraid that others may have some negative opinions about me.
> Q: Did your parents know you did the good deed with your friends?
> A: No, no one knew. I did not tell it to anyone. My parents won't think this is a big deal or at most they may praise me with a few words. Even if I told them, they would respond to it the same as the teacher … would have responded.

Thus, children on the one hand learned from their parents the virtue of humility and followed the instruction of not "showing off" their good deeds and on the other hand had confident negative expectations regarding the way in which their parents would respond to their good deeds in the same manner as their teachers would. It seems that both the parents' teaching about humility and their low or discouraging responses to their children's good deeds shaped children's attitudes and practices concerning lying about good deeds.

THE RULE-GOVERNED STYLE

Chinese children, while arguing for the moral goodness or obligation of not telling the truth about good deeds, expressed a strong orientation toward considering various rules that prescribe how one should behave in certain situations. For a child holding to this rule-governed style, it is virtuous and obligatory to act in accordance with rules that inform one's decision-making in particular settings. The rule-governed style children believed that one who did not publicize or tell the truth about his or her good deeds was doing the right thing because he or she conformed to the rule of right conduct in such settings.

As previously discussed, although more than half of the focal participants made ethical statements of a rule-governed orientation, only two students (a fourth grader and a ninth grader) in the focal sample suggested a predominant rule-governed style of ethical discourse. Therefore, this discussion will be mainly based on these two students' ethical statements, although it will also frequently quote the ethical statements made by other students so as to portray a relatively panoramic view of the rule-governed ethical discourse. This study has found that rules informing the rule-governed ethical discourse include at least four specific forms or variations, including (a) lying about good deeds, (b) discovery, (c) humility or modesty, and (d) learning from role models.

Lying about Good Deeds *per se* as a Rule

The first variation of the rule is lying about good deeds *per se*. For children holding to the rule-governed ethical discourse, "not to report one's good deeds" is the very rule to which one needs to conform while confronting a request to report good deeds. Just as Siqi (9F) said, "Chinese people adhere to such a rule—doing good deeds without leaving one's name." In responding to the question "Why should one deny or conceal his or her good deeds?" the rule-governed style students noted that one is supposed to do so because it is the rule. In other words, lying about good deeds is right or obligatory because lying about good deeds *per se* is the rule of right conduct concerning reporting good deeds.

A total of 22 ethical statements were made that stressed the importance of lying about good deeds as a rule. When asked to tell something about not taking credit for doing good deeds, Jianing (4F) said:

A: Many classmates have done good deeds. Uh...Shijie, for example, has sometimes helped me and sometimes helped others. For example...once I couldn't find my bicycle after school. I was worried about it. I needed my bicycle to go home. Then Shijie lent his to me.
Q: Then how did he himself go home?
A: He lived very close to school and could just walk on foot. Just a few minutes' walk.
Q: Where is your home?
A: Not too far, about 20 minutes' walk.
Q: Did anyone know that Shijie gave his bike to you?
A: No. Shijie did not say anything. In class meetings Shijie did not say anything. Our teacher asked if anyone had good deeds to report, but Shijie did not say anything.
Q: What do you think about Shijie's not reporting his good deed?
A: Oh, he did the right thing. It is right. It is doing good deeds without leaving one's name.

As Jianing's narratives indicate, Shijie's concealment of his good deeds is exactly what he should have done because it conforms to the rule "lying about good deeds," or in Jianing's words, "it is doing good deeds without leaving one's name." She believes that her classmate Shijie (4M) acted appropriately in not reporting his good deed because he conformed to the rule "doing good deeds without leaving one's name" or "lying about good deeds."

Jianing was not alone in such reasoning for the obligation of conforming to the rule "lying about good deeds." Huayue (4M) made the same comment: "It is right that he helped someone else but did not publicize the deed." Clearly, for both Jianing and Huayue, lying about one's good deeds is the rule prescribing how one should decide in the dilemma of lie- or truth-telling about one's good deeds and a rule that one should not break. Therefore, an individual who does not publicize his or her good deeds does the right thing. As fourth graders, Jianing's and Huayue's discourse indicates that they have acquired the basic rule concerning reporting good deeds and have developed the consciousness of conforming to this rule.

As age increased, children's rule-governed ethical discourse became more vivid and was given meaning based on personal understanding. In justifying her judgment, Yuerong (6F) said:

> A: This is doing good deeds without leaving one's name. I think that, while doing a good deed, one just should not leave his name.... It is good that I did good deeds but did not tell others and leave my name.
>
> Q: But it is a good deed. Why not let others know about it?
>
> A: Just because it is a good deed, I was not willing to tell others about it. I think people who conduct good deeds but do not tell others about them are good people.

For Yuerong, lying about good deeds as a rule is no longer merely a rote rule. Instead, it has started to become meaningful and is something that she can think and feel about. When she said "I think..." and "I was not willing to...," lying about good deeds becomes more than a rule one is expected to follow; it becomes something one can base on his or her own reasoning capability. With this rule settled in her mind, Yuerong did not report her good deed even when invited to report; she thinks that the behavior of not reporting a good deed is good and people who do not report their good deeds are good as well.

Yuerong's sentiments were echoed by her classmates. For instance, when the head teacher asked the class to report their good deeds for evaluative purposes, Han (6M) did not report his good deed. When asked what made him not report his deed, he gave a very interesting reply: "Isn't it good to do good deeds without leaving your name? Everybody says that. People who do a good deed do not leave their name are good, because they should not leave their name while doing a good deed." Han's "Isn't it good to…?" suggests that the rule "lying about good deed" is something that he has picked up and a force that has played—continues to do so—a role in his ethical behavior and reasoning.

In addition, when Han said that "everyone says that," he demonstrated that he had accepted it as what everyone else does while at the same time giving lived meaning to the rule. In other words, this rule is not only integrated with Han's lived experience whereby he found "everyone says that," but also internalized as part of his ethical belief: Everyone says that, so it is supposed to be right or good to behave as everyone says. The sixth grader not only adheres to the rule "lying about good deeds," but also begins to base his meaning-making of the rule on his personal lived experience. He no longer simply repeats what the rule prescribes to justify his practical behavior. Instead, he refers to his personal lived experience and constructs knowledge by integrating his personal experience into the understanding of the rule.

However, the ninth graders' discourse varies. Not all ninth graders share the same form of discourse. Some of these students' discourse seems similar to that of the fourth and sixth graders. In the story cited in the first chapter of this book, Bida (9M)—one of the two rule-governed style students in this study—narrated that his classmate Liang caught a thief and was acknowledged by the school, but Liang did not take the credit for doing that good deed when Bida asked him whether it was he who had caught the thief. Bida thought that Liang had acted appropriately and liked the way in which Liang answered his question:

> Q: What do you think made him deny doing the good deed?
> A: Isn't there such a saying (*shuofa*) that to be an unsung hero means doing good deeds without leaving one's name? I also very much appreciate (*zanshang*) this kind of attitude. His denying the good deed seems to me to be very good.

When Bida questioned "Isn't there…," he thought Liang's denying the good deed was good because he followed the commonly recognized rule that if someone wants to be an unsung hero he or she should not admit the good deeds he or she has actually accomplished. For the rule-governed style, lying about good deeds is the rule people should follow. On the other hand, some ninth graders' discourse suggests that people seem to pursue some higher purpose by conforming to the rule of lying about good deeds. Just as Boyuan (9M) said, "There is a noble thought. That is, having helped people but not wanting to tell it, because he felt that he should help that person." It is his belief that people ought to help others; helping others is just like our everyday conduct, nothing unusual, and people just should not tell their good deeds. He further said:

> I would despise them if they take doing good deeds as a means to earn social points…because when you help a person…you should go help him unselfishly, helping someone for the purpose of helping him rather than of achieving some other ends.

Accordingly, doing what one ought to do is just like doing what one does in everyday life and should not be publicized or told to others at all.

Discovery as a Rule

Another variation is what can be called "discovery": The appropriate conduct in a situation of doing good deeds is not to tell one's deed, but to let others find out or discover what one has done. A total of 20 ethical statements were identified that attend to the rule of "discovery" in justifying the moral goodness or obligation of lying about good deeds. As a close reading of these ethical statements reveals, Chinese children believe that the goodness of a good deed consists in its being found out or discovered by others instead of being told to others by the doer of the deed. In other words, it is not good for one to publicize his or her own good deeds; it is better for others to discover or find out what good deeds one has conducted.

Chinese children came to this idea by calculating the cost and benefit of discovery versus telling. Hantong (4M), one of the two strong holders of the rule-governed style, suggests that discovery is the rule that prescribes how one should handle his or her good deeds. He said, "Because if the deed was not found out by others, people themselves usually do not tell others about it.... If it was finally found out by others, it is fine to say whatever one's got to say." Obviously, Hantong calculated the cost and benefit of being discovered by others and being told by the doer of a good deed:

> It is better to be discovered by others than to be told by the doer oneself. It is a little better for the teacher to find out about my good deed. If I do not tell my deed directly, others will still get to know the deed gradually. That is to say, others will gradually discover and know about it. If my classmates noticed what happened and told it to my teacher, my teacher would praise me and I would feel happy to gain praise. It is better to be discovered.

Bida (9M), the other strong holder of the rule-governed style, was even more radically convinced that discovery would add points to one's record if a good deed was discovered by others rather than told by the doer. Let's consider Bida's moral and ethical statements on his classmate Songou's (9M) not reporting his good deed:

> Q: Songou, your classmate, said he helped a lady to the hospital. That lady had been hit by a truck…Songou said he dialed 120 (medical emergency number) and then accompanied the woman to hospital and called her family. Have you ever heard about this?
> A: No, he never told us.
> Q: What do you think about his not reporting his good deed?
> A: I think it is very good.
> Q: What do you think made him not report his good deed?
> A: He did not want our teacher to praise him. He did not want people to think that he was very…uh…anyway…if I were him, I would not have told it, either. Keep silent; let it be found out by others.
> Q: So you think that he did not report his good deed because he wanted others to find it out?
> A: Any way…if he reported his good deed, we would think that he did not want his face (*buyao lian*, or having no sense of shame), saying this in front of so many people.
> Q: So, which do you think, publicizing one's good deed by oneself or letting it be found out by others…?
> A: Publicizing it by oneself is not good. If someone else discovered your good deeds, and then told others—say, your teachers—that you did a good deed…, the teacher would publicize this thing. You will gain a wonderful reputation of "not taking credit (*butu xuming*) for doing good deeds." You can see how wonderful this reputation is. Anyway, I like the way Songou handled his good deed. Even under request, I myself would not tell it, but rather let others find out about it. If others find out about it, it is good. If not, it does not matter.
> Q: Do you mean that, if you were in Songou's situation, you would have behaved as Songou did?
> A: Yes, I would have done the same. Anyway, if it was found out, it would be worth more. It is better to be found out.

As can be seen from this conversation, Bida believes that it is good for people not to report good deeds or publicize one's good deeds. If one's good deed could be discovered by others instead of being publicized by the doer itself, the good deed would be worth more. Therefore, Bida thinks that it is better for one's good deed to be discovered by others than to be told by the doer oneself. He himself was also committed to this rule of discovery, remarking that he would have done the same as Songou if he were in Songou's situation because the way in which Songou handled his good deed conformed to the rule of discovery whereby the doer of a good deed would benefit more—namely, a wonderful reputation of "not taking credit for doing good deeds"—while costing the same—namely, doing a good deed. In contrast, one might benefit less or even hurt his or her reputation if he or she risks telling a good deed to others him- or her-self.

The rule of discovery, as it seems to me, is a rule based on calculating the cost and benefit. However, there could be something more profound underneath this rule: Why should Chinese students think that discovery is better? Here we come to our next rule.

Humility as a Rule

The third variation is the rule of humility or modesty. Humility as a traditional Chinese socio-moral rule has been most frequently cited by existing literature to interpret the socio-cultural mechanism of lying about good deeds. Studies to date believe that Chinese children who commit lying about good deeds are conforming to the rule of humility. However, the psychological dynamics of lying about good deeds, as it seems to me, are far more interesting and complex than what existing literature has suggested.

As determined in the present study, humility is undoubtedly an important rule, but simply one of many that prescribe people's behavior. Of all the 70 rule-governed ethical statements, 18 (25.71%) statements indicated how the rule of humility functioned in children's attitudes and practices of lying about good deeds. However, none of the second graders ever suggested humility or modesty had a significant influence in their discourse; as such, it might still take some time for 7-

year-olds to become familiar with and ultimately pick up humility or modesty as a prescription for social behavior. In comparison, the fourth, sixth, and ninth graders not only showed acquisition of the rule of humility, but also indicated knowledge of its subtlety as to how it might hinder or promote one's reputation.

Commonly agreed by children of the rule-governed style is that people are expected to be humble or modest or to keep low key about one's merit. They made use of the existing rule of humility or modesty as justifications for not telling others about good deeds. In their ethical statements, they repeatedly referred to such words as *humility* or *modesty* as their reasoning or justification for not taking credit for good deeds or doing good deeds without leaving one's name.

Hantong (4M), one of the two strong holders of the rule-governed style, commented that people "might be modest, so they did not tell" about their good deeds. He believed that people did not tell others about their good deeds because they wanted "to be a little modest, a little humble." His classmates also made similar statements that gave weight to the rule of humility or modesty. Xueyue (4F), for example, agreed that a student who deceived his teacher about a good deed may be because he or she wanted to be modest, frequently stating that "he might be modest so he did not tell"; "his deceiving his teacher may be the result of modesty"; "it should be the result of modesty"; "perhaps he is modest and not arrogant"; and "one needs to be humble." These statements suggest that these fourth grade Chinese students have picked up the rule of humility or modesty as it is and made it a guideline for social behavior, for they believed that—as Jiejun (4F) put it—"it is just good…to be a little modest (*qianxu*), a little humble (*xuxin*)."

As children got older, their knowledge of the rule of modesty or humility became increasingly personalized. They came to grips with the subtlety of the rule of humility or modesty in regard to how it will hinder or promote one's reputation. Children used phrases such as "not showing off" or "being low key" instead of 'humility or modesty' to frame their understanding of humility or modesty. For them, to be humble or modest is no longer an abstract socio-moral rule. Instead, they have given life to this abstract rule. Rui (6F) made a very direct statement about the importance of conforming to the rule of humility or modesty, but she did not simply recite her parents' instruction on humility or modesty. "I was taught not to show off...you should not show off when doing a good deed," Rui said, "Doing a good deed is not necessarily worth showing off." Another example is Boyuan (9M), who constructed his own interpretation of humility or modesty. He said, "My principle is to stay low key (*didiao*)," which is "to let you remain quiet."

As we can see, the sixth and ninth graders have turned the rule of humility or modesty, which is abstract for the fourth graders, into a living rule that has been incorporated into their own systems of meanings: either not showing off or staying low key. For them, not telling the truth of one's good deeds is no longer the result of conforming to the rule of humility or modesty. Instead, it has become not only a guideline for their general social behavior, but also part of their mentality that models their behavioral choice within real-life settings.

LEARNING FROM ROLE MODELS AS A RULE

The fourth variation is what I have termed rule "modeling" or "learning from role models." Role models have long been important and useful instruments of socialization and moral education in the society of China. In their story narratives, children frequently referred to role models known for not taking credit for doing good deeds. A total of 10 ethical statements were focused on how role models shaped children's attitudes and practices of lying about good deeds. One widely known role model is Lei Feng, a hero nationally renowned for the magnitude of good deeds unknown to the public until after his death. A movement of "Learning from Lei Feng" was launched in the 1960s, and Chinese people—especially youths—have since been called on to learn from him.

As indicated in focal participants' story narratives, Lei Feng as a role model is still influential in shaping the ethical discourse of Chinese youngsters. The second graders have already been introduced to Lei Feng as a role model who did good deeds without leaving his name. When asked to make a moral statement about whether or not it is right for his classmate Bochao (2M) to lie about his good deeds, Dingzhou (2M) said, "It is right not to tell. He was learning from Lei Feng." It seems to Dingzhou that, although his classmate Bochao did not tell the truth about his good deed, Bochao was doing the right thing, because he conformed to the rule of "learning from Lei Feng," the role model who did not publicize his good deeds.

Although the "Learning from Lei Feng" movement was launched to encourage people to do good deeds for those in need rather than not to publicize their good deeds, Chinese children in the focal sample have come to percieve the meaning of "Learning from Lei Feng" as "doing good deeds without publicizing them." This suggests to some degree that what a society intends to enculturate in its young members might be different than what meaning the youngsters actually construct of the enculturation.

Chinese children's appeal to the rule "learning from role models" is even more apparent in older children's ethical statements. They not only refer to the rule "learning from role models," but also make a well-advised argument for appealing to this rule. Hantong (4M), a strong holder of the rule-governed style, commented on his classmate Shijie's (4M) lying about his good deeds. He said:

> Lei Feng is just this kind of a person who conducted good deeds without making them known to others. Lei Feng did not leave his name when he did good deeds. Shijie behaved like Lei Feng. That is learning from Lei Feng. Shijie was doing the right thing.

What a brilliant argument! A role model, as it seems to this fourth grader, is someone like Lei Feng who conducts good deeds but does not publicize them by himself to mark his name or earn social points. Learning from the role model is doing good deeds without publicizing them. One does the right thing by not telling the truth about a good deed he or she has actually accomplished because that is how role models deal with their good deeds.

Certainly, there are many more role models like Lei Feng, as aired on radio, TV programs, or presented in newspapers, magazines, or textbooks. These roles models could be household heroes who lost their lives while saving others or little guys who simply ran an errand for a senior citizen who could not walk. For example, TV programs talk about either a young migrant worker who saved a bunch of injured people in a traffic accident but left quietly without leaving any personal identification information or a ninth grader who jumped into a frozen lake, saving a drowning little boy but not leaving his name or publicizing his deed before the media found out and made him a role model. We have good reasons to believe that children dwelling in such an atmosphere would refer to role models available everywhere.

THE SOCIAL CONSEQUENTIAL STYLE

The social consequential style is predominantly oriented toward peers' attitudes/responses to truth-telling about good deeds as well as their subsequent effects on one's public image and peer relationship maintenance. As previously mentioned, 24 (58.54%) of the focal sample (n = 41) had predominant awareness of fear and anticipation of peers' negative attitudes and responses to truth-telling about good deeds. These 24 individuals include 3 second graders, 5 fourth graders, 8 sixth graders, and 8 ninth graders. As age increased, children became increasingly concerned about potential interpersonal outcomes of reporting good deeds. When it comes to reporting good deeds, they believe that lying about good deeds can help reduce their vulnerability in an attempt to protect their public image, social network, and harmonious interpersonal relationships.

A fundamental characteristic of the social consequential style consists in a discourse that emphasizes the efficiency and effectiveness of an act in producing the most wanted interpersonal outcomes. Nonetheless, not every child holding to this style appeals to exactly the same form of discourse. In fact, variations in the form of discourse have been identified within five confident negative expectations with regard to peer students' responses to truth-telling, including: (a) peers' distrust, (b) peers' negative evaluation, (c) hurting peer relationship, (d) peers' jealousy, and (e) peers' ridicule or mockery. I will discuss each variation by looking closely at its specific forms of discourse as expressed and represented in children's story narratives and ethical statements.

PEERS' DISTRUST

Peers' distrust in this book refers to children's confident expectations for peer students' skepticism around truth-telling about good deeds. Of the 24 students whose ethical discourse is characteristic of strong social consequential style, 17 (70.83%) reported confident expectations for peer students' distrust. These 17 individuals include 2 fourth graders (n = 11), 7 sixth graders (n = 12), and 8 ninth graders (n = 10). When asked "Why should someone conceal or deny a good deed he or she has accomplished?" these individuals replied with ethical statements featuring social consequential discourse in the form of peers' distrust. Ninety-two ethical statements referring to peers' distrust were made by these students, accounting for 38.83% of all 237 social consequential statements.

Peers' distrust involves two variations. One has to do with children's confident expectation that peers or classmates would be skeptical of the likelihood of a good deed even if they told the truth about their good deeds. It is expressed in the form of students' skepticism as to whether a good deed really exists. This variation is referred to as "peers' distrust of likelihood." The other variation has to do with children's confident expectation that fellow students would question their motives or intentions of doing good deeds if they told others about their good deeds. It is expressed in the form of students' skepticism as to the motives or intentions with which one conducts a good deed. This variation is referred to as "peers' distrust of motives."

The two variations of peers' distrust are slightly different in terms of their respective frequency of being mentioned by the focal participants, with the first variation (i.e., "peers' distrust of likelihood") accounting for 55.43% (51 statements) of the 92 statements and the second variation (i.e., "peers' distrust of motives") accounting for 44.57% (41 statements).

Specifically, "peers' distrust of likelihood" attracted great attention from the fourth and sixth graders in the focal sample. When asked "Why didn't someone tell the truth about his or her good deeds?", the fourth and sixth graders tended to answer with confident expectations for "peers' distrust of likelihood." For instance, Jianing (4F) said, "Generally they (peer students) would say that it is impossible (for me to do good deeds)"; "they don't believe that I did what I did"; "they would feel it is impossible to happen"; and "they believe what they anticipate and do not believe what they did not anticipate." Jianing's comments resonated with those of Yuerong (6F), who said, "Even if you tell it (namely, the truth), others won't believe it. Others will think you are telling lies while you are actually telling the truth. They won't believe you if you tell the truth."

In contrast, "peers' distrust of motives" was frequently mentioned by both sixth graders and—particularly—ninth graders in the focal sample. Children not only expressed confident expectations for peers' distrust of likelihood of a good deed, but also anticipated that peer students would cast strong doubt on one's motives for doing good deeds as a consequence of telling the truth about them. Specifically, children expressed confident expectations that peer students would question the motives of an individual who did, and then publicized a good deed. They expected peer students to suspect that an individual who does a good deed must have some hidden motivation for doing it if he or she publicizes the good deed. They also expected peer students to suspect that someone who publicizes his or her good deeds must want to be praised or earn social points so as to improve one's status and image even though he or she in fact had never thought about it. Fengyuan (9F), in explaining her appraisal of lying about good deeds, stated the following:

> Some people just like to think about others from a negative point. They'd say, "No one saw you do the deed; then you claim you did the good deed, so as to win the teacher's praise." So people just don't want others to say that "on the surface (*biaomianshang*), he/she did the good deed, but in essence, he/she just wanted to be praised." Anyway, people would just think you pretended to do good deeds simply to be praised by the teacher or someone else.

Now the question is about where children obtained this knowledge about peers' distrust. This research study identified two sources. A perhaps minor source has to do with children's belief about the way in which peer students would respond to their truth-telling. Several children said that they themselves did not really experience peers' distrust (because no one would really tell someone their skepticism) but simply assume that peers would cast doubt on truth-telling (because they themselves also tended to be skeptical of other students' good deeds and motives).

The other source has to do with their own lived experience of being distrusted by other students. For example, during a class break, Bida (9M) found a wallet within which there was a relatively large sum of money. Trying to find the person who might have lost the wallet, Bida looked around but did not see anyone. Being unable to find the owner, Bida handed it to a teacher so that the money might be returned to its owner. Bida was praised on the school radio by the principal of the school. When asked whether he ever ran into peer students' distrust, Bida said that several of his classmates teased him, saying that Bida must have handed his own money to the teacher so as to earn praise or moral points.

To determine whether and to what extent Bida's classmates might cast doubt on the likelihood and motives of his doing this good deed, I asked all his classmates who participated in this study (9 students in total) whether they knew about Bida's deed and how they would judge it. These 9 students all remembered that they heard about Bida's deed over the radio, but 7 of them thought either that the money Bida handed to the teacher was his own money or that Bida was seeking praise or reputation by handing in the money. Similar stories were reported happening in other settings. It can be inferred that peers' distrust widely existed in Chinese children's mind and that children came to this perception through lived experiences in the domain of social transaction.

PEERS' NEGATIVE EVALUATION

Peers' negative evaluation refers to children's confident expectation that peer students would negatively evaluate one's truth-telling about his or her good deeds. Of the 24 students holding to the social consequential style, 19 (79.12%) reported confident expectations for peer students' negative evaluation. These 19 individuals include 1 of the second graders (n = 11), 4 of the fourth graders (n = 8), 7 of the sixth graders (n = 12), and 7 of the ninth graders (n = 10). These students made a total of 73 ethical statements referring to peers' negative evaluation, accounting for 30.81% of all 237 social consequential statements. They frequently reported—and appeared to be very sensitive to—peers' negative evaluations of truth-telling about good deeds.

Peers' negative evaluation is associated with two types of concerns. First, children expected peers' negative evaluation to be associated with the weight or importance of a good deed. Since most of the good deeds are what children called "small deeds," they believed that their classmates would ridicule them if a good deed they publicized was not "big" enough. Feixiang (2M) said:

> If you told others about a small deed, they'd say, "Isn't it just a small deed?" They might be thinking why you even dared to report such a small deed. If it is a big deed, they should not say that.

To be sure, a small deed is not necessarily unimportant. Instead, when children refer to a good deed as a small one and thus not worthy of being mentioned to others, it is because they think that most people could do the same deed to help others should they run into it. Just as Rui (6F) said:

> If I tell others about my good deed, which is not necessarily small, some people might still think I am showing off, and they might be thinking, "What the hell makes you show off? Is such a small deed worth telling others? I can also do it if I run into it."

In addition, while children believed that peers' negative evaluations would be based on the centrality of a good deed, it does not mean that a deed of high centrality should be publicized as other factors (e.g., peers' distrust) are being taken into account as well.

Furthermore, peers' negative evaluation is rooted in a belief that everyone has to stay low key so as to keep a good public image. Chinese children reported that, if they told the truth about their good deeds, their classmates would see them as showing off or being hypocritical. Students who reported their good deeds were often accused of showing off, being hypocritical, and wanting to be famous (*xiang chumin*). For example, Lele (6M) said, "If I publicized a good deed, my classmates might say that I was showing off, saying that I was hypocritical, making fame, and wanting to be famous." Haotian (6M) also said, "It (telling the truth about good deeds) makes people feel that you are especially hypocritical."

Although students might so charge others for reporting a good deed, not every student would do so. According to several ninth graders, there are only a few students in each class who are in the habit of "throwing bad words at others." Boyuan (9M) said, "If you tell your teacher your good deeds, you may be viewed as a hypocrite by those who are not very upright." The number of these students is not significant, yet their influences are so strong that one's image might be flawed. As Boyuan said:

> If you tell them about your good deeds, they would mistake you as intentionally showing off. Others will view you very negatively, anyway, that you are very hypocritical. It might also cause others to change their views about you. People might question why you propagandize the deed and why not let it be as it is. That is, your image becomes bad.

Therefore, to avoid peers' negative evaluations and protect one's public image among peer students, one has to shy away from telling others about his or her good deeds.

Children in the focal sample seem to have learned these lessons mainly from their own lived experiences in social transactions. Consider the following conversation between me and a fourth-grade boy named Huayue:

> Q: What if you told your good deed to your teacher?
> A: Classmates would think that I am showing off....
> Q: How do you know that?
> A: Well...once when I was in the second grade, I reported a good deed to my teacher. Then one classmate said I loved to show off and I was hypocritical.
> Q: What have you learned from this experience?
> A: Uh...what I learned is that, if I tell others the truth about my good deed, they will say that I like to show off. If I tell the truth, at most the teacher will praise me a little bit, but my classmates will say bad words about me. If I do not tell my good deed, the teacher will not say anything, and the classmates will not say anything bad about me. Anyway, I just do not want my classmates to say I love showing off.

Living in this type of social environment, students are constantly exposed to peers' negative responses to truth-telling about good deeds. Clearly, students have acquired practical wisdom from their life experience. They have learned the cost of truth-telling and the benefit of lie-telling about good deeds. Life experience has honed their skills in calculating the cost and benefit of lie- and truth-telling about good deeds. They have come to understand that denying a good deed to their teachers would not do much harm while telling the truth is risky because peer students would see them as showing off or being hypocritical, thereby harming their public image among peer students. It can be inferred that it is peers' negative evaluation that has to some extent taught Chinese children the lesson of how to calculate the social consequences for lie- and truth-telling about their good deeds.

HURTING PEER RELATIONSHIPS

Peer relationships matter. As an important form of social consequences, the idea that truth-telling about good deeds would hurt one's relationship with peers was frequently reported by the focal participants. Of the 24 students who expressed a strong social consequential style of ethical discourse, 9 (37.5%) appeared very sensitive to the possible harm that truth-telling about good deeds could bring about related to peer relationships. These 9 individuals (including 3 fourth graders, 3 sixth graders, and 3 ninth graders) made a total of 35 ethical statements (accounting for 14.77% of all social consequential statements) that specifically referred to the negative impact of truth-telling about good deeds on the development and maintenance of healthy peer relationships. Several children of different ages argued for lying about good deeds and expressed their strong concerns about the harm that truth-telling about good deeds might bring about related to interpersonal relationships.

> If I talk about the deed, it is very possible that I won't be able to develop good relationships with my classmates. They will be unhappy with me if I share my deed with the teacher…classmates would be very unhappy with me and would not play with me after class…and I would be isolated by them. I don't want to be isolated; I want to have good relationships with folks.
>
> —Xueyue (4F)

> After class, they will not talk to me if they think I love showing off. And after class, it is your classmates—not your teachers—who will play with you. Whether your teacher praises you or not, the teacher won't play with you. You've got to stay and play with your classmates. You still need your classmates to vote for you if you want to run for any position in your class.
>
> — Lina (6F)

> If you really told the deed to others, then there would be two extremes: some people would think that you helped someone and you are a noble person; others would question why you propagandized it and why not let it be—and in their heart and eyes, your image becomes bad.
>
> —Boyuan (9M)

Obviously, Chinese students considered maintaining good relationships with peer students to be one of the most important tasks in school life. They again calculated the cost of truth-telling and the benefit of lying about good deeds. They were clearheaded about who—classmates or teachers—were more important for their days spent at school. They realized that their classmates would not play with them after class even if teachers praised them for their good deeds and that classmates would become unhappy and even angry with those who shared their good deeds with the teachers, thereby isolating them after class. Chinese children concluded that behaviors that might do harm to peer relationships should be avoided and behaviors that might help develop and improve interpersonal harmony are desirable. In regard to reporting good deeds, children believed that truth-telling about good deeds harms relationships with peers and should be avoided and that lying about good deeds is preferred as it improves or at least does no harm to their public image and interpersonal harmony.

PEERS' JEALOUSY

Children were worried that, if they reported their good deeds and received praise from their teachers, classmates would become jealous. A total of 9 students—including 1 first grader, 4 fourth graders, and 4 sixth graders—made 27 ethical statements that expressed their concern about peer students' jealousy of both their good deeds and subsequent praise or rewards. For example, Dongyu (2M) cleaned up his classroom but denied that it was he who did it when his teacher asked him. In explaining why he did not take the credit for a good deed, he said, "If I told the truth, my classmates would do this deed next time before I could do it because they also wanted to be praised." Dongyu clearly expected that his classmates who also wanted to be praised by teachers would steal future opportunities to do voluntary cleaning of the class from him.

To be sure, Dongyu's strategy does not necessarily function as well as he wishes, but it does suggest that the contest starts from an early stage of life among Chinese students. It was suggested by some focal participants that Chinese children from the school days were taught by their parents to compete with classmates in all aspects of school life so as to secure advantages over others. This competition-driven jealousy became increasingly intense among older children, who were faced with increasingly intense competition around every aspect, which could ultimately impact one's opportunity of going to a "better" (in the sense of academic achievement) school. As Lina (4F) said, "My classmates will think that today you conducted good deeds and got praise from the teacher, so tomorrow I will do more good deeds." Lina, who was about 9 years old when we met, had come to realize that, by doing good deeds and becoming a teachers' pet, students would undoubtedly add points to their contest for better opportunities. For Lina, lying about good deeds would lead other students to think that she did not attempt to edge others out of the contest whereas truth-telling would risk her chance of standing out in the contest.

This competition-driven jealousy could also bring about danger or harm to one's physical safety. Zhihao (6M) suggested that each class had students who were jealous of others' merits and would spare no pains to make trouble if they became jealous of someone. As he put it, "For those whose sense of jealousy is strong, they might make trouble for you when they one day take a certain powerful position in the class." In order to avoid such potential troubles, one must be very cautious of becoming the target or victim of peers' jealousy. Yawen (9F) said, "The classmates become jealous if you are praised for doing good deeds. Classmates just will not like it if you get praised by the teacher, because they also want to be praised and become teachers' favorite students." To avoid becoming a victim of peers' jealousy, lying about one's good deed is certainly a better choice than truth-telling. Just as Songou (9M) said, "Because he did not tell the truth to the teacher, this would help him avoid his classmates' jealousy." With all this in mind, children have good reasons for preferring lying to truth-telling about their good deeds as few would want to take the risk of being the target of destructive jealousy.

Peers' Ridicule or Mockery

Peers' ridicule or mockery emerges in the form of either making a face or teasing. Oftentimes children would make fun of their classmates who reported good deeds to their teachers. Peers' ridicule or mockery is also considered in Chinese children's cost-benefit calculation in moral conflicts, although—in comparison with the previously mentioned forms of social consequential discourse—peers' ridicule is not as frequently reported by participants. Specifically, of the 24 strong holders of the social consequential ethical discourse style, 4 children (16.67%) expressed confident expectations that peer students would make fun of them if they told the truth about their good deeds. These 4 individuals—including 1 second grader, 2 fourth graders, and 1 sixth graders—made 10 statements that suggested strong expectations that peers would ridicule them for truth-telling about good deeds. These statements account for just 4.22% of the social consequential statements. As indicated by the focal participants, peers' ridicule might not be really ill-meant, but the ridiculed would feel uncomfortable or sometimes embarrassed. Peers' ridicule naturally prompts children to take steps to reduce their vulnerability in an attempt to protect themselves from being hurt. For those who are sensitive to peers' ridicule, lying about good deeds is certainly an effective step of self-protection.

THE EXPRESSIVE STYLE

The expressive style of ethical discourse is mainly oriented toward going with one's feelings resulting from emotions, sentiments, and desires. For the expressive style, personal feelings matter. It is good to go with one's affective state of consciousness. Not telling the truth about one's good deeds is good if it is accorded with what he or she feels good doing. It is good to keep a good deed from being known to others only if doing so satisfies one's desire, optimizes one's emotional experiences, or makes one feel good. As previously discussed, of the 41 focal participants, 7 students' ethical discourse carried the predominant characteristic of the expressive style—namely, going with feelings. These 7 individuals include 2 second graders, 2 fourth graders, and 3 sixth graders. It was further found that several ninth graders made expressive ethical statements, but none suggested a predominant orientation toward the qualities of personal feelings related to reporting good deeds. Surely, this does not mean that the ninth graders do not "go with their feelings"; rather, it simply implies that they have other more compelling considerations (e.g., social consequences of threat to peer relationships) when it comes to reporting good deeds.

An outstanding characteristic of the expressive style is its going-with-feelings discourse. In responding to the question "Why not tell the truth about one's good deeds?", the expressive style typically gives priority to personal impulsive emotions, sentiments, and desires. The words *want*, *feel*, and *like* were mostly frequently mentioned by those demonstrating the expressive style. As indicated in their ethical statements, similar forms of discourse are employed, such as "I just did not want to tell them"; "I just feel it is good not to tell the truth"; "He did not want to tell others the truth"; and "I generally don't like to tell my things to others." For instance, Tao (2M) explained why he did not tell the truth about his good deeds, suggesting a strong sense of going with the feelings. He said, "I don't want to tell"; "I feel I should not tell"; and "I feel it is good not to tell."

Certainly, this basic form of discourse also indicates some subtle variations, and not every child of the expressive style employed the same phrasing. Specifically, variations in the form of discourse were found within three affective states of consciousness: (a) psychological self-satisfaction; (b) embarrassment; and (c) the desire to fulfill a personal right. In deliberating each of these variations, I will focus on the specific discourse forms represented in the ethical statements of the 7 strong holders of the expressive style while simultaneously making use of other students' comments.

SELF-SATISFACTION

Self-satisfaction is the feeling we have when we are satisfied with ourselves or with our accomplishments; it is the contentment we feel when we have fulfilled our desires, needs, or expectations. When asked "Why should one not tell the truth about the good?", children of the expressive style answered by turning to their affective consciousness of psychological self-satisfaction. For instance, Xinyu (4F) explained why her classmate Xueyue (4M) lied about his good deed, saying, "He may be thinking about leaving honor to others and, for himself, what matters is that he feels comfortable." Furthermore, Haotian (6M) stated:

> It is psychologically satisfying (*xinlishang manzu*) for me to help a stranger, so there is no need to publicize it. Keeping quiet gives you more spiritual satisfaction. If you tell others about your good deeds, you will psychologically feel very annoyed. If you don't talk about the deed, you will feel very happy and satisfied in your inner heart.

All 7 children embodying the expressive style carried strong consciousness of self-satisfaction around lie- or truth-telling about good deeds. Of all the 94 expressive ethical statements, 59 (accounting for 62.77%) highlighted the priority of psychological self-satisfaction for determining children's attitudes and practices of lying about good deeds.

Children's expressive discourse suggests that it is just as bad to go against satisfying one's own feelings as to tell others one's good deeds. Two levels of psychological self-satisfaction come into play. One level consists of the satisfaction that children feel with themselves for doing good deeds, such as helping others. For one who holds to the expressive style, doing a good deed to help others is a behavior that goes with one's feelings and makes him or her feel happy and comfortable in being capable to help others. Xueyue (6M) said:

> Doing a good deed makes you feel happy. Doing a good deed makes ourselves feel so happy. There is no need to tell others. We did the good deed with the thought of "helping others for happiness (*zhurenweile*)."

Clearly, it is the act of "doing good deeds" *per se* that makes Xueyue feel good as this helps him fulfill his desire to help others who are in the moment of need. In short, children feel happy or satisfied with themselves for being able to fulfill their desire to help others.

The second level of psychological self-satisfaction that comes into play relates to not telling others about one's good deeds. Wanyu (6F) said,

> You should not talk about the deed you did. Anyway, if you do not propagandize it, you will feel very happy in your inner heart, because you helped someone. Although people nay not know about what you did, your heart would feel satisfied with it, feel happy…feel happy for your deed because, as a child, you are able to help others.

Obviously, not taking credit for her good deeds helps Wanyu fulfill her desire which drives her to do the good deeds and thus makes her feel satisfied with herself. In contrast, sharing her good deeds with others would hurt her sense of happiness or self-satisfaction as a result of feeling her capability to help others. In other words, when a good deed is publicized, her sense of self-satisfaction grounded in the desire to help others is damaged as the original motivation of doing the good deed is simply to fulfill her desire to help others rather than make the act itself known to the public.

EMBARRASSMENT

Embarrassment is a nearly universal human emotion that unfolds in front of us as a form of social pain along with the confusion or disturbance of mind when one's incapability or guilt is made public (Harris, 2006). A slightly tortured smile, an averted gaze, and the telltale blush are all recognized signs of embarrassment. Four of the 7 holders of the expressive style expressed strong concerns about potential embarrassment as a result of truth-telling about good deeds. They said, "I will feel very embarrassed if I tell my good deeds to others"; and "I will not tell the truth, as I will be embarrassed." Of the 94 expressive ethical statements, 20 (21.28%) suggested strong affective consciousness of embarrassment related to reporting good deeds. For children of the expressive style, telling their good deeds to others made them feel embarrassed.

The idea that telling the truth about one's good deeds can make one feel embarrassed sounds somewhat inconceivable unless we listen to the inner voice of the child to discover the story behind the scenes. As indicated by focal participants' story narratives, their embarrassment stems from at least two sources. One source of their embarrassment seems to be related to their own sense of shame in being unable to conform to the precepts of right conduct. For instance, Bida (9M), although a strong holder of the rule-governed style, made very impressive expressive statements concerning such sensitivity to shame. Explaining why he did not tell others about his good deed, Bida said, "If I tell others about my good deeds, then I will feel embarrassed. I will feel I am extremely, extremely shameless. I myself will even look down upon me." It is noteworthy that Bida's strong opposition to truth-telling about good deeds and his related lying about good deeds to one's sensitivity to shame might be associated with his rule-governed style of ethical discourse. For Bida, truth-telling about good deeds violates the rule that one should not take credit for doing good deeds; the violation of this rule gives rise to one's sense of shame in being unable to adhere to the rule. In other words, this expressive form of discourse related to embarrassment seems to be rooted in the rule-governed style of discourse which stresses the need to conform to precepts of appropriate behavior.

Another source of children's embarrassment is their expressive discourse, which mingles with considering social consequences. As previously discussed, Chinese culture is often considered a "shame culture" in which people are explicitly expected to be sensitive to conditions fostering shame and to other people's opinions, judgments, and evaluations. When asked "Why not tell the truth about a good deed?", children of the expressive style answered it by considering social consequences or peers' responses. For instance, Wanyu (6F) had a strong expressive style of discourse. She recalled her experience when she did not tell her teacher about her good deed. One day on her way to school, she helped an injured old lady get to the hospital and was thus late for school. When her teacher questioned her about the reason for her tardiness,[17] instead of telling the truth about her good deed, she simply replied that she overslept and got up late. In explaining her rationale for not telling the truth, Wanyu said:

> If I tell my good deeds to my teacher, my teacher may praise me, and I will become the center of people's discussion. People will say I am "begging for praise" and "love to showing off." I will feel embarrassed.

In Chinese society, a prevalent social expectation is that people who conduct good deeds should not take the credit for doing the deeds; as a result, people are expected to feel embarrassed about failing to meet this social expectation. Wanyu's ethical statements show how the Chinese culture has shaped her mentality, particularly her ethical discourse.

Desire to Fulfill a Personal Right

It was initially somewhat surprising when a fourth-grade Chinese student named Xinyu (4F) said that, when her teacher asked her to acknowledge a good deed she had accomplished, she did not share her good deeds because she believed she had the right to keep silent and wanted to fulfill her right. I was subsequently able to spot more such moments when the focal participants discussed their desire to fulfill a personal right as a justification for not sharing their good deeds with teachers or classmates.

The three children who demonstrated the expressive discourse style expressed the desire to fulfill a personal right to keep silent or not tell others about

[17] It should be noted that, in most of the stories, carrying out a good deed did not "cost" the doer; however, in stories like this one, doing the good deed made Wanyu late. The present study did not have much data to explain these two kinds of situation. Future efforts should take a closer look at this issue.

their good deeds when faced with requests to report good deeds. Specifically, of all 94 expressive ethical statements, 9 (9.57%) emphasized the right to make a personal choice not to publicize one's good deeds. Although this is certainly not a significant number compared to that of "self-satisfaction" or "embarrassment," this discourse of attending to the desire to fulfill a personal right deserves some particular attention.

For instance, when Lele (6M) said that, "I just do not want to tell; I think I have the right to keep silent," he was suggesting that he wanted to satisfy his desire that commanded him not to talk about his good deed with his teacher. He might have realized that it was not sufficient for him to defend his choice of not telling the teacher about his good deed if he simply attended to his personal desire. Therefore, he turned to his belief that as an individual he had the right to keep silent, refusing to answer questions or respond to requests that he felt went against his desire.

Another sixth grader, Lina (6F), had a similar theory. She thought that it was good for her classmate Lele to lie about a good deed and that she herself would do the same as Lele did. When questioned why she perceived this as a good approach, she said, "Because he wants to do so. It is his choice. I feel it is ok to keep it to you. He has the right." Thus, Lina's argument starts with the human "want" whereby one can be driven; when she realizes that satisfying one's desire does not always make a good argument, she ends her argument with the concept of "right," which few could deny of a human being.

CHAPTER 5
Discussion, Implications, and Suggestions

It is as though explorers keep reporting the existence of a hitherto unknown animal, but their fragmentary glimpse of it convinces them that they are observing different creatures.

— P.N. Johnson-Laird (1983)

Creating, yet not possessing. Working, yet not taking credit. Work is done, then forgotten. Therefore it lasts forever.

— Lao Tzu (1989)

DISCUSSION

This inquiry began with a general goal of searching out the modes of Chinese children's ethical discourse in order to expand our current knowledge about and understanding of the "mental steps" (Sigel, 1985, p. 346) leading to Chinese youngsters' attitudes toward and practical behaviors related to lying about good deeds. Anchored in a narrative approach, this study solicited and examined Chinese children's encounters with and attitudes toward reporting good deeds in real-life settings. I sought to determine what considerations went into lying about good deeds. In so doing, this study was able to focus on listening to individuals' inner voices that empower them to take one action rather than another. This effort has captured some of the dynamic interplays between children's lived experience and narratives, unpacking the multiple dimensions of Chinese children's ethical discourse on lying about good deeds.

SOURCES OF MORAL KNOWLEDGE: INSTITUTIONAL VS. NON-INSTITUTIONAL

Chinese children were constantly exposed to institutional attitudes and recommended practices with regard to reporting good deeds. Not only did youngsters receive purposeful instructions and formative evaluations from family and social authority regarding how to behave properly in the dilemma of whether or not to publicize their good deeds, but they were also systematically socialized to socio-moral rules through constant exposure to school curricula, extracurricular activities, newspapers, magazines, and radio or TV programs that honored role models—national or local—who did not take credit for helping others or serving their communities. This observation of institutional sources of knowledge is consistent with existing literature (e.g., Bond et al., 1982; Davin, 1991; Lassiter, 1998; Lee et al., 1997, 2001; Price, 1992), which has documented that both Chinese families and schools spare no pains socializing young generations to traditional socio-moral rules (e.g., humility, modesty) of appropriate conduct.

Chinese children were also frequently exposed to non-institutional, yet influential sources of practical wisdom through peer interactions. They attached great importance to the attitudes and responses of peer students or friends within the same social network. They considered knowledge obtained and constructed through peer interactions to be genuine guidance for social and moral decision-making. Chinese children recollected the discouraging or disparaging ways in which peer students responded to individuals who took credit for their good deeds. From these daily peer interactions, Chinese youngsters constructed meaningful knowledge that informs them how they ought to act in real-life settings. This knowledge ultimately became a non-institutional discourse governing or justifying children's evaluative and behavioral decisions of lying about good deeds.

This observation provides direct evidence that children's social interactions with peer students contributed as much as—if not more than—institutional efforts did to the construction of children's ethical discourse. As Piaget (1950) said, "Human knowledge is essentially collective and social life constitutes one of the essential factors in the formation and increase of pre-scientific and scientific knowledge" (cited in Kitchener, 1991, p. 429). I believe that social orientation takes part in Chinese children's moral knowledge construction, which is consistent with Piaget's (1932/1965) argument that imposed morality can never be genuine morality and genuine morality is constructed in the context of peer interactions.

ETHICAL DISCOURSE: CONSISTENCY VS. CONTROVERSY

Chinese children's ethical discourse entails at least four major styles: authoritative, rule-governed, social consequential, and expressive. Although each of these styles has distinctive features, they are shaped by the entire dynamic character of Chinese socio-moral culture and form a compatible, integrated moral structure that shapes the individuals' ethical decision-making. As an example of this holistic yet complex character, a child's ethical discourse is usually characterized by a dominant mode while simultaneously sharing some of the features of other styles.

The authoritative style. Chinese children's ethical discourse is characterized by an orientation toward the attitudes and responses of teachers and parents. This finding is consistent with the earlier discussion about the role of social and family authority in shaping Chinese character and behavior, although it provides little evidence for the speculation about the role of political authority.

This absence of political authority in children's discourse does not necessarily imply that there is anything wrong with the present study or Wen's (2005) conceptualization of social, family, and political authority in Chinese society. Wen's work is based on the general Chinese socio-moral culture and particularly applies to adults. The present study is focused on 7- to 15-year-olds who are basically living under the wings of parents and teachers and for whom political authority in general has yet to become a concern.

In comparison with those of parents, schoolteachers' attitudes and responses seem to play an overwhelming role in children's justifications for not reporting good deeds. This is not to suggest that parents' attitudes and responses are not important for children's ethical decision-making. We should consider the reality that children's lying about good deeds more often occurs in school or similar social settings than in family settings. Understandably, they are more likely to attend to teachers' attitudes and responses and show less concern about those of parents. I believe that it is not only authority itself, but also the settings in which a certain behavior occurs that have shaped children's authoritative discourse. A child's authoritative discourse is rooted in the Chinese cultural emphasis on obedience to authority as well as based on his/her construal of a specific context.

The rule-governed style. Chinese culture emphasizes the importance of complying with the law of right conduct for maintaining interpersonal harmony. Chinese children's ethical discourse entails an orientation toward conforming to social-moral rules of right conduct relating to reporting good deeds. These rules include not only traditional socio-moral rules explicitly taught in Chinese families and schools (e.g., humility, learning from role models), but also those that children constructed in the context of peer interactions (e.g., discovery). This finding expands our conceptualization of Chinese people's conformism to traditional socio-moral rules of proper behavior.

The finding that only a very small proportion of the participants in the present study hold to the rule-governed style of ethical discourse does not provide adequate support for existing literature. For instance, Fu et al. (2001) and Lee et al. (1997, 2001) suggested that Chinese children's positive attitudes toward not telling the truth about good deeds were to large extent due to their conforming to the traditional Chinese socio-moral rule of humility or modesty. Studies to date have pointed to the rule-governed dimension of Chinese children's ethical discourse, yet they obviously failed to draw as full a picture as the four-dimension panorama the current study presents of Chinese children's ethical discourse.

The social consequential style. Chinese culture is a relational culture. People living in this culture are considered to be relational beings, characterized by a strong tendency to consider the social consequences an act would bring about for the maintenance of harmonious interpersonal relationships. In the present study, the majority of the fourth, sixth, and ninth graders were overwhelmingly concerned about peers' attitudes and responses to truth-telling about good deeds. The proportion of students holding to the social consequential style even exceeded that of those who belong to the other three styles of ethical discourse. The prevalence of the social consequential style among Chinese children suggests the extent to which Chinese teenagers have become relational beings. It provides direct evidence in support of our initial assumption that the relational elements of Chinese culture would factor into the construct of children's ethical discourse on lying about good deeds.

Existing literature (Fu et al., 2001; Lee et al., 1997, 2001) suggests that lying about good deeds is essentially rooted in children's rule-governed ethical discourse. This rule-justification perspective contradicts what has been found in the present study. The theory of self-vs.-others discrepancy provides one plausible explanation for this controversy. In the present study, participants' moral judgment and justification were mainly grounded in their own moral experiences in real-life settings. According to Saltzstein (1994) as well as Turiel and Wainryb (1993), I have good reason to believe that children in the present study would—consciously or unconsciously—tend to defend and justify their own decisions by highlighting their social consequences of threats to social or peer interactions. In existing studies, participants without exception made moral judgments and justifications about story characters' moral decisions that would do little or no harm to the participants' well-being. While making evaluative decisions on others' behaviors, participants would primarily consider whether and to what degree such behaviors comply with or violate relevant rules. In this sense, the controversy over the roles of considering social consequences and complying with various rules is an issue of self-vs.-others in rule application. This dimension of rule application was not accounted for in approaches employed by other researchers.

The expressive style. Chinese society has been known for its long tradition of emphasizing the control of individuals' feelings. This tradition has recently witnessed the "going-with-the-feelings" change emerging among Chinese people, particularly youngsters. This new trend, which highlights free expression of personal feelings and the assertion of a person's rights, seems to be represented in the ethical discourse of Chinese children. A small proportion of the children in the present study suggested a strong expressive orientation, considering both the quality of personal emotional experiences (e.g., personal right of choice, embarrassment, and psychological self-satisfaction) and the protection of individual rights (e.g., the right to keep silent) in moral decision-making. A good number of the children who are not strong holders of the expressive style have also referred to personal feelings as justifications for not telling the truth about good deeds. This finding is to some extent consistent with the previous discussion with regard to how the recent social transformation and reformation in the society of China has reshaped Chinese youngsters' expression of emotions, desires, and wants.

In addition, this study has found that students of the expressive style are mostly fourth and sixth graders whose discourse primarily takes the forms of expressive words, phrases, and short sentences. This is unlike the social consequential style, for example, whose discourse is usually expressed and represented in long sentences and sometimes runs as long as a fully developed essay. However, it remains unclear whether and to what degree children, while participating in the present study, tried to reserve or control their feelings. What is for sure, however, is that the majority of the study participants seldom talked in length about personal feelings. This might be due to either the difficulty they might encounter in talking about personal emotional experiences or the residuals of the traditional emphasis on the control of expressing personal emotions, desires, and wants.

SOCIAL INTERACTIONS: AUTHORITY VS. PEERS

There appears to be an authority-vs.-peers discrepancy characterizing the ethical discourse of Chinese children. Overall, second graders revealed a strong authoritative orientation toward the attitudes and responses of social and family authority. Fourth, sixth, and ninth graders were mainly oriented toward peers' attitudes and responses. This authority-vs.-peers discrepancy might be understood in terms of what Habermas (1990) distinguished between symmetric and asymmetric social interactions. In asymmetric social interactions, the interacting individuals differ in status, authority, and/or power. The moral perspectives of the individuals who are in higher status and who have authority and/or power may be privileged over the moral perspectives of those who are in lower status and who have little or no authority and/or power. Meanwhile, the interacting individuals in symmetric social interactions are equal parties in communication and have no authority and/or power to impose their moral perspectives on one another. All the parties in symmetric social interactions are involved in discourse, debate, and argumentation of equality and freedom. They are very likely to be involved in genuine coordination and reflection, which facilitate the development of trust and friendship.

In Chinese society, social interactions between children and parents or between students and teachers are considered asymmetric. The moral perspectives of adults are understandably privileged over those of youngsters. Social interactions between children and their peers approximate the ideal of symmetric social interactions. In peer interactions, no single party has absolute authority or power to impose its moral perspectives on other parties. Plausibly, peer interactions become settings in which genuine meaning-making is most likely to occur. Peers' attitudes and responses function as formative forces that shape and model a child's evaluative and behavioral decisions in moral conflicts.

For the relatively young children, such as the 7-year-old second graders in the present study, their interactions with parents and teachers are asymmetric. In socio-moral dilemmas, they tend to obey adults' instructions because they are sensitive to adults' attitudes and responses to their behaviors. As children get older, such as the fourth, sixth, and ninth graders in this inquiry, they have more and more opportunities to engage in various interactions with peer students and friends. These interactions are in essence symmetric as all parties involved in these interactions are equal stakeholders or game players. Without exception, they are not expected to have authority or power to impose their perspectives on others. For older children, peer interactions are more comfortable than interactions with parents and teachers. With increased experience in symmetric social interactions, older children tend to give priority to peers' attitudes and responses in determining whether or not to report their good deeds.

Social Distrust: Performance vs. Self-Protection

Social distrust is "the confident expectation that another individual's motives, intentions, and behaviors are sinister and harmful to one's own interests" (Lewicki & Tomlinson, 2003). Chinese children's ethical discourse entails a strong sense of social distrust, which seems to exist universally among students. Not only does a child distrust that others have told the truth even when they do, but the child also distrusts that others would trust him or her even if he or she tells the truth. Furthermore, the social distrust expressed in children's ethical discourse seems present between students and teachers. Students distrust that their teachers are really interested in their good deeds and that their teachers would trust them even if they tell the truth. Meanwhile, teachers distrust that their students have told the truth even when students have in fact told the truth. Mired in a milieu of social distrust, Chinese children believe that, in order for them to be trusted or avoid being distrusted, the best possible way is to deny, conceal, or not admit the good deeds they have in fact performed as they believe it is much easier for them to win teachers' trust when they tell lies than when they tell the truth.

Lying about good deeds could be viewed as a self-protection strategy, one that helps protect a child from being distrusted by teachers and peer students. Just as Lewicki and Tomlinson (2003) pointed out, within interdependent relationships, social distrust often "entails a sense of fear and anticipation of discomfort or danger" and "naturally prompts us to take steps that reduce our vulnerability in an attempt to protect our interests." I believe that many Chinese children—if not all—deny or lie about their good deeds mainly because they consider it to be a strategy for reducing their vulnerability in social interactions, particularly asymmetric interactions. This strategy keeps them from being harmed by others' distrust, thereby helping them maintain a positive public image and construct strong social networks.

This finding is the first in the literature to provide direct evidence that lying about good deeds might be a self-protection strategy for many individuals. Yet it contradicts Bakken's (2000) argument that Chinese people practice lying about good deeds simply because they want to become "good" in the eyes of others. Bakken posits that lying about good deeds is simply a type of performance or "simulation" whereby one pretends to be someone one is actually not (p. 422). Bakken may be right to some degree. At least the two students who demonstrated the rule-governed style in the current study believe that lying about good deeds is right because lying about good deeds *per se* is the rule of right conduct in the situation of reporting good deeds.

That being said, there is no denying that social distrust has a long history in Chinese society and is still prevalent nowadays. According to Lian (1993), social distrust among Chinese people is deeply rooted in the heritage of Han Fei (also Han Feizi), an influential thinker in the third century BCE. For instance, Han Fei argued that a ruler should trust neither his ministers nor subjects, neither his kin nor his closest friends. He believed that the ministers appointed by a ruler may try to gain power in order to pursue their own personal aims. A wise ruler must enact laws to ensure that the ministers fulfill their duties and that all ministers comply with the ruler's authority. Being a minister himself, Han Fei actually claimed that he himself cannot be trusted either. Han Fei's theorization of social distrust, along with his other teachings, has influenced Chinese society for more than 2000 years.

Social distrust in Chinese society has been strengthened by social and political events on various occasions. A recent example is the notorious 1957 "All schools of thoughts speak up and all flowers of colors blossom" movement. During that time period, the late Chinese leader Mao Zedong (or Mao Tse-tung) first called upon intellectuals to speak their inner voices, including their criticisms of the Chinese Communist Party and its regime. Those who did speak out were subsequently sent to work on "Labor Reforming Farms," the so-called Chinese Gulag Archipelago, as a penalty. The last two or three decades have further witnessed a dramatic increase in the level of daily social distrust in China. Claims have surfaced that Chinese society is experiencing a crisis of trust. People try to find covert meanings in others' behaviors and intentions. Interpersonal communication is often distorted even though messages are meant to be honest and candid. It is commonly agreed that re-establishing the value of interpersonal trust has become an urgent mission from which people of truthfulness and sincerity cannot escape.

IMPLICATIONS

Moral issues, by any standard, are complex and are made more so as they vary with culture (Murphy, 2008). This study examined the phenomenon of not telling the truth about doing a good deed. Chinese social policy and school curriculum place a high value on anonymous good deeds, which in this official paradigm reflect the socially desired values of social responsibility and modesty and the negative values of fame seeking and individual distinction. Although study participants were sensitive to this official ideal, their motivations to conform to it varied. Overall, the present study contributes to the existing literature in four major aspects.

Chinese children's story narratives related to lying about good deeds indicate that multiple dimensions (rather than a single dimension, as suggested by previous studies) feature in Chinese children's ethical discourse. This multiple-dimension paradigm of ethical discourse expands our current knowledge about the mental steps leading to Chinese children's attitudes toward and practices of lying about good deeds. It may also be used as a suggestive model for the exploration and interpretation of other social and moral issues existing or emerging in Chinese society.

Through this study I was able to identify four styles of Chinese children's ethical discourse by applying a narrative-based approach to the topic. Without examining the rich and complex narratives of the participants, a multi-dimensional understanding of children's ethical discourse is almost unimaginable. To some extent, this study exemplifies how a narrative approach, through examination of personal meaning-making of lived experiences in real-life settings, could help disclose the richness and complexity of personal inner worlds to which other research approaches may have had little access. Surely, I do not want to suggest that the narrative approach employed in this study is all that is necessary for the study of complex developmental or social issues. Rather, by adopting a research approach radically different from those repeated in existing studies, I have been able to draw a more rounded, multifaceted picture of the cognitive, affective, and conative dimensions of Chinese children's ethical discourse.

Recommended practices give rise to discourse, which subsequently enters into the formation of one's moral autonomy. In educational practice, educators and educational institutions should handle what we teach with great caution. We ought to pay particular attention to the ways in which our instruction may be received and interpreted by young generations. For instance, in Chinese society, the teaching of humility or modesty is certainly not meant to plant in the evolving mind of young generations the idea that they should lie about their achievement or good deeds. Nevertheless, what children make out of this teaching is always different than what society originally hoped. Another example is the instruction of "Learning from Lei Feng." Chinese society hopes that its young members will behave like Lei Feng and always be ready to help others; however, students have learned, as suggested in their narratives, that they should help others and not talk about their good deeds to other people because Lei Feng is always presented as someone who performed many good deeds but never publicized them.

The finding that Chinese children's ethical discourse contains at least four major ideal styles is consistent with Tipton's (1982, 2002) four-style framework of American ethical discourse. This consistency might provide some evidence in support of the speculation that a multi-style framework of ethical discourse could be cross-culturally applicable. There is no denying that my four styles of Chinese children's ethical discourse contain different socio-cultural elements than Tipton's four styles of American ethical discourse. However, I believe that we both have revealed that differences in individuals' attitudes and practices related to specific behavioral decisions are in essence rooted in variations in the way people react to authority, rules, consequences, and personal affective consciousness.

SUGGESTIONS

After several years of exploration in a complex field such as Chinese children's ethical discourse on lying about good deeds, I have come to realize that it is almost impossible to unpack all the problems through a single research study. To be sure, many issues deserve further exploration. I would like to suggest that at least the following three issues deserve extensive research efforts in the future.

A most important finding of the present study is that concern about social consequence of moral acts (in the sense of peers' attitudes and responses) is a dominant motivation among the majority of Chinese children, particularly older ones. This finding contradicts findings in previous literature that conforming to socio-cultural rules dominates Chinese children's ethical discourse. As discussed earlier in this chapter, this controversy might stem from the difference in the research approaches taken by the present study and previous studies. However, it remains unclear whether and to what degree differences in research approaches have contributed to the controversy over the roles of social consequence and socio-cultural rules in determining youngsters' moral decision-making. Future research might find it promising to look into this issue.

Another meaningful finding of the present study is the age differences of dominant ethical discourse style. The authoritative style dominated the ethical discourse of the second graders while the social consequential style dominated that of the fourth, sixth, and ninth graders. This finding is based on the data produced by a relatively small sample of students who were attending the same primary school or high school in the same city of Beijing. Although each child may construct different meanings from similar schooling experiences, they may also have similar patterns of discourse based on these similar experiences. Furthermore, the finding is based on cross-sectional data. It is unclear whether and to what degree this pattern will still hold true among longitudinal data gathered from the same age group at different periods of time. For future efforts, in addition to longitudinal data, securing a relatively large sample comprising participants from different geographical areas and different schools might bring about results to further solidify the findings of the present study.

Finally, another interesting finding—the prevalence of social distrust in Chinese society and in Chinese children's ethical discourse—deserves extensive research efforts. With its main focus on searching for the styles of Chinese children's ethical discourse, the present study did not look specifically at the issue of social distrust, which should be specifically explored for its own sake. In fact, social distrust could be a very promising research area. Social distrust is ubiquitous in China, existing in the business world, the political arena, and many (if not all) relationships. What is different is in what ways and to what degree people in different settings and relationships practice and experience social distrust.

Although for some social distrust offers potentially valuable benefits, social distrust overall has adverse effects (Lewicki, McAllister, & Bies, 1998). Taken to its extreme, it can give rise to paranoid cognitions—false or exaggerated cognitions that one is subject to malevolent treatment by others. Such perceptions drive individuals to the point of hyper-vigilance. People try to make sense of every action that another person takes, brooding on the meaning of others' behaviors and intentions. Such excessive social distrust often leads to a faulty diagnosis about whether the other can be trusted or not. Communication becomes less effective as a means of extricating the parties from the conflict as messages are assumed to be distorted or deceptive rather than honest and candid. Thus, future researchers might find it theoretically promising and practically meaningful to investigate, for example, the impacts of social distrust on youngsters' efforts to establish and maintain healthy social networks in real-life settings.

Appendices

APPENDIX A: THE QUESTIONNAIRE

ID #: ________________

Thank you for participating in this study. This questionnaire includes a series of questions which ask about your beliefs, your feelings, and your experiences with doing good deeds. All your answers will be confidential. This means that your answers will not be shared with your parents, teachers, classmates, friends, or anyone else without your permission. Your answers will only be reported in group form and will, therefore, be completely anonymous. Your answers will help the researchers better understand Chinese children's social and moral development.

Please be as honest as possible. This is not a test and you will not be "graded" on it. There is no right or wrong answer; just answer what it is true for you. If there is any question you do not understand, please raise your hand and I will come help you. On this first page, please print your name and the name of your school below. There tear off this sheet from the rest of the survey. That way your name will not be with your survey responses.

- Your Name: ____________
- Your School: ___________

Now, please tear this page off from the rest of this survey. Please do not write your name anywhere else on the survey. Thank you, and please begin.

ID #: ____________

1. My birthday is (   ) Year (   ) Month (   ) Day.
2. I am (   ) a girl; or (   ) a boy.
3. Do you have siblings? If yes, how many?
4. What do your parents do to make a living?
5. Does your family own an apartment or rent it? How many rooms are there?
6. When you say someone conducts a good deed, what is a good deed? (Example)
7. Please fill in the following parenthesis with: A = Good; B = Bad; C = No Idea.
    a. Hit neighbor's window glass. (   )
    b. Help parents with housework. (   )
    c. Help cleaning the blackboard during a class break. (   )
    d. Bringing home others' belongings without permission. (   )
    e. Drug abuse. (   )
    f. Smoking cigarette. (   )
    g. Help ill strangers to hospital. (   )
    h. Bullying schoolmates. (   )
    i. Donating money to areas hit by natural disasters. (   )
    j. Not telling the truth. (   )
    k. Cheating on exam. (   )
    l. Reporting classmates' misbehaviors to teachers. (   )
8. Were you ever praised for doing good deeds?
9. Have you ever told others about the good deeds you did?
10. Have you ever read or heard about stories of someone who conducted good deeds to help others?
11. Do you know any story of "doing good deeds without leaving one's name?"
12. A. Lulin, on his way to school, actively helped a stranger who accidentally injured his ankle to the hospital.

    Question: Do you think what Lulin did is good or bad?

    B. Thus Lulin was late when he arrived at school. His teacher asked him why he was late. He answered that he missed the bus.

Question: Do you think what Lulin said to his teacher is good or bad?

13. A. Xiaojia helped with tidying up the classroom during a class break while her classmates and teacher were outside.

    Question: Do you think what Xiaojia did is good or bad?

    B. When her teacher found someone cleaned up the classroom, she happened to ask Xiaojia whether she knew who did the good deed. Xiaojia replied that she did not know who did it and she did not do it

    Question: Do you think what Xiaojia said is good or bad?

14. Are you interested in participating in other research tasks in which I will interview you (20-30 minutes for each interview)? Yes (   ); No (   )

APPENDIX B: INDIVIDUAL INTERVIEW PROTOCOL NO. 1

RAPPORT

1. Thanks for his/her participation in the study;
2. Re-introduce the purpose of the study and what I hope to learn;
3. Emphasize the point that there is no right or wrong answer;
4. Discuss issues of confidentiality;
5. Ask for permission to tape-record;
6. Ask if the participant has any question.

SAMPLE QUESTIONS: CONTEXT OF PERSONAL LIVED EXPERIENCES

1. Have you ever done a good deed to someone?

2. (If yes) Tell me what happened.
3. Did other people know that you helped someone?
4. (If yes) How did they get to know what you did?
5. (If no) Why did not you tell others what you did?
6. Were you ever troubled with whether or not to tell others that you helped someone?
7. Were you ever worried about whether you should tell others about your good deeds?
8. Were you ever worried that people would never know about your good deeds if you did not tell others?
9. Do you know anyone in your school or class who conducted good deeds without making his or her good deeds known to others?
10. (If yes) Tell me what happened
11. Or do you remember any story you read or heard about in which a person did good deeds but did not admit his or her good deeds?
12. (If yes) Tell me what happened

Closing Questions

1. Anything else to tell me before we end today's interview?
2. Thank you again for participating today's interview.

APPENDIX C: INDIVIDUAL INTERVIEW PROTOCOL NO. 2

RAPPORT

1. Thanks for his/her participation in the study;
2. Re-introduce the purpose of the study and what I hope to learn;
3. Emphasize the point that there is no right or wrong answer;
4. Discuss issues of confidentiality;
5. Ask for permission to tape-record;
6. Ask if the participant has any question.

SAMPLE QUESTIONS: RECONSTRUCTING PERSONAL LIVED EXPERIENCES

1. Tell me a story in which you helped others.
   1) What happened?
   2) What is next?
   3) How did you feel about yourself when doing the good deeds?
   4) It is a neat story. Can you tell me more?
2. Did you let anyone know your good deeds?
   1) What made you decide to tell or not to tell your good deeds to others?
   2) What would happen if you told? Why?
   3) What would happen if you did not tell? Why?
3. Do you know a story in which some did good deeds to others, the community, or schools?
   1) What happened?
   2) What is next?

3) How did you feel about him or her?
4) How do you feel would she or he feel about?
5) It is really a neat story. Can you tell me more?

4. How did you know that person conducted the good deeds?
    1) What would happen if s/he told others his/her name and/or what she did?
    2) What would happen if s/he didn't tell his/her name and/or what she did?
5. Do you think the person should tell what he did to others? Why or why not?

Closing Questions

1. Do you have anything more to bring up or to ask about before we end our conversation?
2. Thank you again for participating in the study.

APPENDIX D: GROUP INTERVIEW PROTOCOL

Rapport

1. Thanks for his/her participation in the study;
2. Re-introduce the study (share the purpose of the study and what I hope to learn);
3. Emphasize the point that there is no right or wrong answer;

4. Discuss issues of confidentiality and instruct participants to keep group discussion information confidential, not to mention it to any non-group members;
5. Ask for permission to videotape;
6. Ask if the participant has any question.

SAMPLE QUESTIONS

1. How many of you ever helped others?
2. Did anyone know that you help others?
3. How did he or she know it?
4. *Or why didn't you tell others your good deeds?*
5. How many of you have ever heard about someone who did good deeds?
6. How did you know it?
7. What happened to him or her after other people knew his or her good deed?
8. Who can tell me a story you read in which a person did good deeds?
9. What is it about? Did the person tell others his or her good deeds?
10. Do you think he or she should (or should not) tell others his or her good deeds? Why do you think so?

CLOSING QUESTIONS

1. Do you have anything else to tell me before we end today's interview?
2. Thank you all again for participating today's interview.

Bibliography

Aiken, H. D. (1952). The level of moral discourse. *Ethics, 62*(4), 235-248.

Arendt, H. (1972). *Crises of the republic.* New York, NY: Harcourt Brace Jovanovich.

Aronson, E., Wilson, T. D., & Akert, A. M. (2005). *Social psychology* (5th ed.). Upper Saddle River, NJ: Prentice.

The Associated Press. (2007, August 21). *Beijing's environment shows strain as population passes 17 million.* Retrieved from http://climate.weather.com/articles/strains082107.html

Bakken, B. (2000). *The exemplary society: Human improvement, social control, and the dangers of modernity in China.* New York: Oxford University Press.

Bedford, O., & Hwang, K. K. (2003). Guilt and shame in Chinese culture: A cross-cultural framework from the perspective of morality and identity. *Journal for the Theory of Social Behavior, 33*(2), 127-144.

Behar, R. (1990). Rage and redemption: Reading the life story of a Mexican marketing woman. *Feminist Studies, 16*(2), 223-259.

Benedict, R. (1946). *The chrysanthemum and the sword: Patterns of Japanese culture.* New York, NY: New American Library.

Benton, R. J. (1982). Political expediency and lying: Kant vs. Benjamin Constant. *Journal of the History of Ideas, 43*(1), 135-144.

Blum, S. D. (2007). *Lies that bind: Chinese truth, other truths.* New York, NY: Rowman & Littlefield Publishers, Inc.

Bodde, D. (1953). Harmony and conflict in Chinese philosophy. In A. F. Wright (Ed.), *Studies in Chinese thought.* Chicago, IL: University of Chicago Press.

Bok, S. (1979). *Lying: Moral choice in public and private life.* New York, NY: Vintage Books.

Bond, M. H. (1986). *Lifting one of the last bamboo curtains: Review of the psychology of the Chinese people.* Hong Kong, China: Oxford University Press.

Bond, M. H. (1993). Emotions and the expression in Chinese culture. *Journal of Nonverbal Behavior, 17*(4), 245-262.

Bond, M. H., & Hwang, K. K. (1986). The social psychology of Chinese people. In M. H. Bond (Ed.), *The psychology of the Chinese people* (pp. 213-266). Oxford, UK: Oxford University Press.

Bond, M. H., Leung, K., & Wan, K. C. (1982). The social impact of self-effacing attributions: The Chinese case. *Journal of Social Psychology, 118*, 157-166.

Bortolussi, M., & Dixon, P. (2003). *Psychonarratology: Foundations for the empirical study of literary response*. New York, NY: Cambridge University Press.

Bruner, E. M. (1986). Experience and its expression. In V. W. Turner & E. M. Bruner (Eds.), *The anthropology of experience* (pp. 3-30). Chicago, IL: University of Illinois Press.

Cao, D. (1999). "Ought to" as a Chinese legal performative. *International Journal for the Semiotics of Law, 12*, 153-169.

Carson, T. L. (2006). The definition of lying. *Noûs, 40*(2), 284-306

Chang, C. (1960) Chinese intuitionism: A reply to Feigl on intuition. *Philosophy East and West, 10*(1/2), 35-49.

Chase, P. G. (2006). *The emergence of culture: The evolution of a uniquely human way of life*. New York, NY: Springer.

Chen, Z. Z. (1989). The theoretical analysis and practical study of the psychology of face. In K. S. Yang (Ed.), *The Psychology of the Chinese* (pp.155-237). Taipei: Guiguan Tushu Gongsi Chubanshe.

Chipman, L. (1971). The ascriptive character of ethical discourse. *Ethics, 81*(4), 326-331.

Chisholm, R. M., & Feehan, T. D. (1977). The intent to deceive. *Journal of Philosophy, 74*, 143-159.

Chu, G. C. (1967). Sex differences in persuasibility among Chinese. *International Journal of Psychology, 2*, 283-288.

Cohen, R. (1997). *Negotiating across cultures: Communications obstacles in international diplomacy*. Washington DC: U.S. Institute of Peace Press.

Coleman, L., & Kay, P. (1981). Prototype semantics: The English verb 'lie'. *Language*, 57, 26-44.

Congressional-Executive Commission on China. (n.d.). *China's household registration system: Sustained reform needed to protect China's rural migrants*. Retrieved from http://www.cecc.gov/pages/news/hukou.php.

Crapanzano, V. (1980). *Tuhami: Portrait of a Moroccan*. Chicago, IL: University of Chicago Press.

Csikszentmihalyi, M., & Rathunde, K. (1998). The development of the person: An experiential perspective on the ontogenesis of psychological complexity. In W. Damon (Series Ed.) & R. M. Lerner (Vol. Ed.), *Handbook of child psychology: Vol. 1. Theoretical models of human development* (5th ed., pp. 635-684). New York, NY: Wiley.

Curran, J. (2005). *Modes of moral discourses in the preferential option for the poor*. Unpublished doctoral dissertation, Boston College, Boston, Massachusetts.

D'Andrade, R. G. (1992). Schemas and motivation. In R. G. D'Andrade & C. Strauss (Eds.), *Human motives and cultural models* (pp. 23-44). New York, NY: Cambridge University Press.

Davin, D. (1991). The early childhood education of the only child generation in urban China. In I. Epstein (Ed.), *Chinese education: Problems, policies, and prospects* (pp. 42-65). New York, NY: Garland.

Denzin, N. K. (1978). *The research act: A theoretical introduction to sociological methods*. New York, NY: McGraw Hill.

Duckworth, E. (Ed.). (2001). *"Tell me more": Listening to learners explain*. New York, NY: Teachers College Press.

Eastmond, M. (2007). Stories as lived experience: Narratives in forced migration research. *Journal of Refugee Studies, 20*(2), 248-264.

Edwards, C. P. (1985). Rationality, Culture, and the Construction of "Ethical Discourse": A Comparative Perspective. *Ethos, 13*(4), 318-339.

Edwards, P. (1955). *The logic of moral discourse*. Glencoe, IL: Free Press.

Ekman, P. (1985). *Telling lies: Clues to deceit in the marketplace, politics, and marriage*. New York, NY: Norton & Company.

Erll, A. (2009). Naïve, repetitive, or cultural: Options of an ethical narratology. *Amsterdam International Electronic Journal for Cultural Narratology, 5*. Retrieved from http://cf.hum.uva.nl/narratology/a09_Erll.htm.

Fang, G., Fang, F-X, Keller, M. A., Edelstein, W., Kehle, T. J., & Bray, M. A. (2003). Social moral reasoning in Chinese children: A developmental study. *Psychology in the Schools, 40*(1), 125-138.

Fairbank, J. K. (1966). How to deal with the Chinese revolution. *The New York Review of Books, 6*(2), 12.

Fairbank, J. K. (1980, September 07). China: The center of the world. *China: Advertising Supplement to the San Francisco Examiner*, 12-14.

Fingarette, H. (1972). *Confucius: The secular as sacred*. New York, IL: Harper Torchbooks.

Fivush, R., & Hudson, J. (Eds.). (1990). *Knowing and remembering in young children*. New York, NY: Cambridge University Press.

Foucault, M. (1972). *The Archeology of Knowledge*. (A. M. Sheridan-Smith, Trans.). London, UK: Tavistock.

Foucault, M. (1978). *The history of sexuality* (Vol. 2). New York, NY: Pantheon.

Foucault, M. (1988). *Madness and civilization: A history of insanity in the age of reason*. New York, NY: Random House.

Foucault, M. (1997). On the genealogy of ethics: An overview of work in progress. In P. Rabinow (Ed.), *Ethics: Subjectivity and truth* (pp. 255-80). (R. Hurley, Trans.). New York, NY: The New Press.

Fu, G., Lee, K., Cameron, C. A., & Xu, F. (2001). Chinese and Canadian adults' categorization and evaluation of lie- and truth-telling about prosocial and antisocial behaviors. *Journal of Cross-cultural Psychology, 32*(6), 720-727.

Fung, H. (1999). Becoming a moral child: The socialization of shame among young Chinese children. *Ethos, 27*(2), 180-209.

Gadamer, H. (1975). *Truth and method*. London, UK: Sheed & Ward.

Gilligan, C. (1977). In a different voice: Women's conceptions of self and morality. *Harvard Educational Review, 47*, 481-517.

Gilligan, C. (1982). *In a different voice: Psychological theories and women's development.* Cambridge, MA: Harvard University Press.

Gilligan, C., & Attanucci, J. (1988). Two moral orientations: Gender differences and similarities. *Merrril-Palmer Quarterly, 34*(3), 223-237.

Gilligan, C., Brown, L., & Rogers, A. (1990). Psyche embedded: A place for body, relationships, and culture in personality theory. In A. I. Rabin, R. Zucker, R. Emmons, & S. Frank (Eds.), *Studying persons and lives*. New York: Springer.

Gold, T. B. (1993). Go with your feelings: Hong Kong and Taiwan popular culture in Mainland China. *The China Quarterly, 136*, 907-925.

Goldfarb, J. C. (1989). *Beyond Glasnost: The Post-Totalitarian Mind.* Chicago, IL: University of Chicago Press.

Grice, H. P. (1975). Logic and conversation. In P. Cole & J. L. Morgan (Eds.), *Syntax and semantics: Vol. 3. Speech acts* (pp. 41-58). New York, NY: Academic Press.

Gustafson, J. M. (1990). Moral discourse about medicine: A variety of forms. *The Journal of Medicine and Philosophy, 15*, 125-142.

Habermas, J. (1990). *Moral consciousness and communicative action.* Cambridge, MA: MIT Press.

Han, J. J., Leichtman, M. D., & Wang, Q. (1998). Autobiographical memory in Korean, Chinese, and American children. *Developmental Psychology, 34*(4), 701-713.

Harkness, S., & Super, C. M. (Eds.). (1996). *Parents' cultural belief systems.* New York, NY: Guilford.

Hsiao, K. C. (1954). *A history of Chinese political thought.* Taipei: Chung-Hua Wen-Hua Chu-Pan She.

Hsu, F. L. K. (1948). Conformity and character. *American Psychologist, 10*, 191-198.

Hsu, F. L. K. (1953). *Americans and Chinese: Two ways of life*. New York, NY: Schuman.

Hsu, F. L. K. (1971). Psychological homeostasis and jen: Conceptual tools for advancing psychological anthropology. *American Anthropologist, 73*, 23-44.

Hu, H. C. (1944). The Chinese concept of "face." *American Anthropologist, 46*, 45-64.

Huang, L. C., & Harris, M. B. (1973). Conformity in Chinese and Americans: A field experiment. *Journal of Cross-cultural Psychology, 4*(4), 427-434.

Johnson, J. (2005). *What is discourse?* Retrieved from http://www.stolaf.edu/depts/cis/wp/johnsoja/whatisdiscourse/index.html

Johnson-Laird, P. N. (1983). *Mental models: Toward a cognitive science of language, inference, and consciousness*. Cambridge, MA: Harvard University Press.

Kao, S. C., & Landreth, G. L. (2000). Play therapy with Chinese children: Needed modification. In G. L. Landreth (Ed.), *Innovations in play therapy: Issues, process, and special populations* (pp. 43-50). New York, NY: Routledge.

Kaplan, J. P., & Green, G. M. (1995). Grammar and inferences of rationality in interpreting the child pornography statute. *Washington University Law Quarterly, 73*(3), 1223-1252.

Kelly, G. A. (1955). *The psychology of personal constructs.* New York, NY: Norton.

Kitchener, R. F. (1991). Jean Piaget: The unknown sociologist? *The British Journal of Sociology, 42*(3), 421-442.

Kleiman, A., & Lin, T. Y. (Eds.). (1981). *Normal and abnormal behavior in Chinese culture* (pp. 17-136). Boston, MA: D. Reidel Publishing Company.

Krefting, L. (1991). Rigor in qualitative research: The assessment of trustworthiness. *American Journal of Occupational Therapy, 45*, 214-222.

Kupfer, J. (1982). The moral presumption against lying. *Review of Metaphysics, 36*, 103-126.

Kvale, S. (1996). *Interviews: An introduction to qualitative research interviewing.* Thousand Oaks, CA: Sage Publications.

Lakoff, R. (1973). The logic of politeness: Or minding your P's and Q's. In *Papers Presented at the Ninth Regional Meeting of the Chicago Linguistic Society* (pp. 292-305). Chicago, IL: Chicago Linguistics Society.

Lamarque, P. (1990). Narrative and invention: The limits of fictionality. In C. Nash (Ed.), *Narrative in culture: The uses of storytelling in the sciences, philosophy, and literature* (pp. 131-153). London, UK: University of Warwick Center for Research in Philosophy and Literature.

Lao Tzu. (1989). *Tao Te Ching.* (G. F. Feng & J. English, Trans.). Vintage Books. Retrieved from http://www.terebess.hu/english/tao/gia.html.

Lassiter, S. M. (1998). *Cultures of color in America: A guide to family, religion and health.* Westport, CT: Greenwood Press.

Lee, K. (2000). Lying as doing deceptive things with words: A speech act theoretical perspective. In J. W. Astington (Ed.), *Minds in the making: Essays in honor of David R. Olson* (pp. 177-196). Malden, MA: Blackwell Publishers.

Lee, K., Cameron, C. A., Xu, F., Fu, G., & Board, J. (1997). Chinese and Canadian children's evaluations of lying and truth telling: Similarities and differences in the context of pro- and anti-social behaviors. *Child Development, 68*(5), 924-934.

Lee, K., Xu, F., Fu, G., Cameron, C. A., & Chen, S. (2001). Taiwan and Mainland Chinese and Canadian children's categorization and evaluation of lie- and truth- telling: A modesty effect. *British Journal of Developmental Psychology, 19*, 525-542.

Lewicki, R. J., & Tomlinson, E. C. (2003). Distrust. In G. Burgess & H. Burgess (Eds.), *Beyond Intractability.* Retrieved from http://www.beyondintractability.org/essay/distrust/

Lewicki, R. J., McAllister, D. J., & Bies, D. J. (1998). Trust and distrust: New relationships and realities. *Academy of Management Review, 20*, 709-734.

Li, J. (2002). A cultural model of learning: Chinese "heart and mind for wanting to learn." *Journal of Cross-cultural Psychology, 33*(3), 248-269.

Lian, G. T. (1993). *Zhongguoren de zhen mianmu (The real Chinese people).* Taibei: Qian wei chu ban she (Avon Guard Publishing Company)

Liang, S. M. (1974). *Chung-kuo wen hua yao-i* (The essential features of Chinese culture). Hong Kong, China: Chi-Cheng T'u-Shu Kung Hsu.

Lightfoot, C., & Valsiner, J. (1992). Parental belief systems under the influence: Social guidance of the construction of personal culture. In I. E. Sigel, A. V. McGillicuddy, & J. J. Goodnow (Eds.), *Parental belief system: The psychological consequences for children* (2nd ed., pp. 393-414). Hillsdale, NJ: Lawrence Erlbaum Associates.

Lin, Y. S. (1974-1975). The evolution of the pre-Confucian meaning of jen and Confucian concept of moral autonomy. *Monumenta Sinica, 31*, 172-204.

Lincoln, Y. S., & Guba, E. G. (1985). *Naturalistic inquiry*. Beverly Hills, CA: Sage Publications.

Lu, L. (2001). Understanding happiness: A look into the Chinese folk psychology. *Journal of Happiness Studies, 2*, 407-432.

Ma, H. K. (1988). The Chinese perspective on moral development. *International Journal of Psychology, 23,* 201-227.

MacIntyre, A. (1981). *After virtue: A study in moral theory*. South Bend, IN: University of Notre Dame Press.

Mahon, J. E. (2008). Two definitions of lying. *International Journal of Applied Philosophy, 22*(2), 211-230.

Markus, H. R., & Kitayama, S. (1991). Culture and the self: Implications for cognition, emotion, and motivation. *Psychological Review, 98* (2), 224-253.

Maxwell, J. A. (1996). *Qualitative research design: An interactive approach.* Thousand Oaks, CA: Sage Publications.

Miles, M., & Huberman, A. (1984). *Qualitative data analysis: A sourcebook of new methods*. Beverly Hills, CA: Sage Publications.

Montaigne, M. (1952). *The essays of Michel de Montaigne*. (C. Cotton, Trans.; W. C. Hazlitt, Ed.). Chicago, IL: Encyclopædia Britannica. (Original work published 1572).

Moore, C. A. (1967). Introduction: The humanistic Chinese mind. In C. A. Moore (Ed.), *The Chinese Mind.* Honolulu, HI: University of Hawaii Press.

Moore, M. C. (1987). Ethical discourse and Foucault's conception of ethics. *Human Studies, 10*(1), 80-95.

Murphy, J. A. (2008, March 04). *Official paradigm and individual variation* (personal email communication).

Nash, C. (1994). *Narrative in culture*. London, UK: Routledge.

Nelson, K. (1996). *Language in cognitive development: The emergence of the mediated mind.* New York, NY: Cambridge University Press.

Nyberg, D. (1993). *The vanished truth: Truth telling and deceiving in ordinary life*. Chicago, IL: The University of Chicago Press.

Orwell, G. (1961). *Collected Essays*. London, UK: Secker & Warburg.

Parsons, T. (1961). Culture and the social system: Introduction. In T. Parsons, E. Shils, K. D. Naegele, & J. R. Pitts (Eds.), *Theories of society: Foundations of modern sociological theory* (Vol. 2, pp. 963-993). New York, NY: The Free Press.

Perkins, D. (1992). *Smart schools: From training memories to educating minds*. New York, NY: The Free Press.

Perkins, S. J. (1999). *Globalization—The people dimension: Human resources strategies for global expansion*. Dover, NH: Kogan Page.

Piaget, J. (1965). *The moral judgment of the child.* (M. Gabain, Trans.). New York, NY: The Free Press. (Original work published 1932).

Piaget, J. (1950). *Introduction a l'épistémologie génétique: Vol. III. La Pensée biologique, la pensée psychologique et la pensée sociologique*. Paris, France: Presses Universitaires de France.

Potter, J., & Wetherell, M. (1987). *Discourse and social psychology: Beyond attitudes and behaviors*. London, UK: Sage Publications.

Potter, R. B. (1965). *The structure of certain American Christians' views on nuclear dilemma.* Unpublished doctoral dissertation, Harvard University, Cambridge, Massachusetts

Price, R. (1992). Moral-political education and modernization. In R. Hayhoe (Ed.), *Education and modernization: The Chinese experiences* (pp.221-238). New York, NY: Pergamon.

Ricoeur, P. (1992). *Oneself as another.* (K. Blamey, Trans.). Chicago, IL: University of Chicago Press. (Original work published 1990).

Ricoeur, P. (1983). *Temps et récit*. Paris, France: Seuil.

Rogers, C. (1969). *Freedom to learn*. Columbus, OH: Merrill.

Rosenberg, S. (2004). Face. In G. Burgess & H. Burgess (Eds.), *Beyond Intractability*. Conflict Research Consortium, University of Colorado, Boulder. Available from http://www.beyondintractability.org/essay/face/.

Saltzstein, H. D. (1994). The relation between moral judgment and behavior: A social cognitive and decision-making analysis. *Human Development, 37*, 299-312.

Sanders, C. J. (1991). Liberation ethics in the ex-slave interviews. In D. N. Hopkins & G. C. Cummings (Eds.), *Cut loose your stammering tongue: Black theology in the slave narratives* (pp. 103-136). Marynoll, NY: Orbis Books.

Schoenhals, M. (1993). *The paradox of power in a People's Republic of China's middle school*. Armonk, NY: M. E. Sharpe.

Schutz, A. (1972). *The phenomenology of the social world*. London, UK: Heineman.

Schwandt, T. A. (2001). *Dictionary of qualitative inquiry* (2nd ed.). Thousand Oaks, CA: Sage Publications.

Seidman, I. (1998). *Interviewing as qualitative research*. New York, NY: Teachers College Press.

Serban, G. (2001). *Lying: Man's second nature*. Westport, CT: Praeger.

Shibles, W. (1985). *Lying: A critical analysis.* Whitewater, WI: The Language Press.

Sigel, I. E. (1985). A conceptual analysis of beliefs. In I. E. Sigel (Ed.), *Parental belief systems: The psychological consequences for children* (pp. 345-371). Hillsdale, NJ: Lawrence Erlbaum Associates.

Singer, M. (1971). *Educated Youth and the Cultural Revolution in China.* Ann Arbor, MI: University of Michigan, Center for Chinese Studies.

Skultans, V. (1999). Weaving new lives from an Old Fleece: Gender and ethnicity in Latvian narrative. In R. Barot (Ed.), *Ethnicity, gender, and social change* (pp. 169-190). New York, NY: Palgrave.

Solomon, R. H. (1971). *Mao's revolution and the Chinese political culture.* Berkeley, CA: University of California Press.

Spiro, M. E. (1987). Collective representations and mental representations in religious symbol systems. In B. Kilborne & L. L. Langness (Eds.), *Culture and human nature* (pp. 161-184). Chicago, IL: University of Chicago Press.

Strauss, C. (1992). Models and motives. In R. G. D'Andrade & C. Strauss (Eds.), *Human Motives and Behavior: Publications of the Society for Psychological Anthropology* (pp. 1-20). Cambridge, UK: Cambridge University Press.

Strauss, A., & Corbin, J. (1998). *Basics of qualitative research: Techniques and procedures for developing grounded theory.* Thousand Oaks, CA: Sage Publications.

Sutton-Smith, B. (1981). *The folkstories of children.* Philadelphia, PA: University of Philadelphia Press.

Sweetser, E. E. (1987). The definition of lie: An examination of the folk models underlying a semantic prototype. In D. Holland & N. Quinn (Eds.), *Cultural models in language and thought* (pp. 43-66). New York, NY: Cambridge University Press.

Tappan, M. B. (1989). Stories lived and stories told: The narrative structure of late adolescent moral development. *Human Development, 32*, 300-315.

Tappan, M. B. (1990). Hermeneutics and moral development: Interpreting narrative representations of moral experience. *Developmental Review, 10*, 239-265.

Tappan, M. B. (1991). Narrative, language, and moral experience. *Journal of Moral Education, 20*(3), 243-256.

Tappan, M. B., & Packer, M. (Eds.) (1991). Narrative and Storytelling: Implications for understanding moral development. *New Directions for Child Development, 54.* San Francisco, CA: Jossey-Bass.

Tillman, H. C. (1987). Consciousness of t'ien in Chu Hsi's thoughts. *Harvard Journal of Asiatic Studies, 47*(1), 31-50.

Tipton, S. M. (1982). *Getting saved from the sixties: Moral meaning in conversion and cultural change.* Berkeley, CA: University of California Press.

Tipton, S. M. (2002). Social differentiation and moral pluralism. In R. Madsen, W. M. Sullivan, A. Swidler, & S. M. Tipton (Eds.), *Meaning and modernity: Religion, polity, and self* (pp. 15-40). Berkeley and Los Angeles, CA: University of California Press.

Tu, W. M. (1974). Reconstructing the Confucian tradition. *Harvard Journal of Asiatic Studies, 33(3)*, 446.

Tucker, E (1995). Tales and legends. In B. Sutton-Smith, J. Mechling, T. W. Johnson, & F. R. McMahon (Eds.), *Children's folklore: A source book* (pp. 193-211). New York, NY: Garland.

Tudor-Hart, B. E. (1926). Are there cases in which lies are necessary? *Pedagogical Seminary, 33*, 586-641.

Turiel, E., & Wainryb, C. (1993). *Social reasoning and the varieties of social experiences in cultural contexts*. Berkeley, CA: University of California Berkeley.

Valsiner, J. (1988). Ontogeny of co-construction of culture within socially organized environmental settings. In J. Valsiner (Ed.), *Child development within culturally structured environments* (Vol. 2, pp. 283-297). Norwood, NJ: Ablex Publishing Corporation.

Vrij, A. (2000). *Detecting lies and deceit: The psychology of lying and the implications for professional practice.* Chichester, UK: John Wiley & Sons.

Wang, C. C. (2008, January 06). *Chinese traditional culture and morality* (personal phone communication).

Wang, F. L. (2005). *Organizing through division and exclusion.* Stanford, CA: Stanford University Press

Wang, F. Y. (2004). Confucian thinking in traditional moral education. *Journal of Moral Education, 33*(4), 430-447.

Wang, Q., & Leichtman, M. D. (2000). Same beginnings, different stories: A comparison of American and Chinese children's narratives. *Child Development, 71*(5), 1329-1346.

Wang, S. (1992). *Wo shi Wang Shuo (I am Wang Shuo).* Beijing, China: Beijing International Cultural Press.

Wen, C. Y. (2005). Chinese national Character: A value-orientation perspective (cong jiazhi quxiang tan zhongguo guominxing). In Y. Y. Li & K. S. Yang (Eds.), *The Personality of the Chinese (zhongguo ren de xingge)* (pp. 40-71). Nanjing, China: Jiangsu Education Publishing House.

White, H. (1981). The values of narrativity in the representation of reality. In W. J. T. Mitchell (Ed.), *On narrative* (pp. 1-24). Chicago, IL: Chicago University Press.

Wilson, R. W. (1970). *Learning to be Chinese*. Cambridge, MA: MIT Press.

Wilson, R. W. (1974). *The Moral state: A study of the political socialization of Chinese and American Children.* New York, NY: The Free Press.

Wilson, R. W. (1981). Conformity and deviance regarding moral rules in Chinese society: A socialization perspective. In A. Kleiman & T. Y. Lin (Eds.), *Normal and abnormal behavior in Chinese culture* (pp. 117-136). Boston,

MA: D. Reidel Publishing Company.

Wright, A. F. (1962). Values, roles and personalities. In A. F. Wright & D. Twitchett (Eds.), *Confucian personalities* (pp. 3-32). Stanford, CA: Stanford University Press.

Xavier, N. S. (2006). *Fulfilling heart and soul: Meeting psychological and spiritual needs with conscience*. Bloomington, IN: AuthorHouse.

Yang, B. J. (1960). *Mengzi yizhu (Translated notes on Mencius).* Beijing, China: Zhonghua Book Company.

Yang, B. J. (1980). *Lunyu yizhu (Translated notes on The Analects of Confucius).* Beijing, China: Zhonghua Book Company.

Yang, K. S. (1981). Social orientation and individual modernity among Chinese students in Taiwan. *Journal of Social Psychology, 113*, 159-170.

Yao, Y. S. (2004). The elite class background of Wang Shuo and his hooligan characters. *Modern China, 30*(4), 431-469.

Yu, T. H., & Wen, W. C. (2004). Monologic and Dialogic Styles of Argumentation: A Bakhtinian Analysis of Academic Debates between Mainland China and Taiwan. *Argumentation, 18*(3), 369-379.

Zhu, W. Z. (1992). Confucius and traditional Chinese education: An assessment. In R. Hayhoe (Ed.), *Education and modernization: The Chinese experience* (pp. 3-22). New York, NY: Pergamon Press.

Zhu, Z. X. (Ed.). (1982). *Issues in child developmental psychology* (in Chinese). Beijing, China: Beijing Normal University Press.

Index

D

E

F

G

H

M

N

Minghui Gao

Dr. Minghui Gao is an Assistant Professor of Education in the Department of Teacher Education at Arkansas State University. Dr. Gao obtained his Ed.D. from Harvard University Graduate School of Education in Cambridge, Massachusetts.